The Founders, the Consti
Public Administration

The Founders, the Constitution, and Public Administration
A Conflict in Worldviews

Michael W. Spicer

GEORGETOWN UNIVERSITY PRESS / WASHINGTON, D.C.

Georgetown University Press, Washington, D.C.   20007
© 1995 by Georgetown University Press. All rights reserved.
10   9   8   7   6   5   4   3   2   1   1995
THIS VOLUME IS PRINTED ON ACID-FREE OFFSET BOOKPAPER.

Library of Congress Cataloging-in-Publication Data

Spicer, Michael W.
    The founders, the Constitution, and public administration : a
conflict in world views / Michael W. Spicer.
        p.   cm.
    1. Public administration--United States--History.   2. Political
science--United States--History.   3. United States--Constitutional
history.   I. Title.
JA84.U5S66   1995
350'.000973--dc20
ISBN 0-87840-581-X (cloth). -- ISBN 0-87840-582-8 (paper)
                                                              94-32279

To Three Arthurs:
my late father, Arthur Spicer;
my son, Jeffrey Arthur Spicer;
and my good friend and colleague, Arthur B. Murphy

Contents

Preface

This book is about how public administration writers look at the world and the problems this creates for our thinking about the role of public administration in American governance. Perhaps because my own formal education was in large part in the "dismal science" of economics, I have often been struck by the distinctively optimistic and frankly almost utopian view of human nature and government exhibited by many of my colleagues in public administration; a view that is quite different from that held by the typical economist. This difference in worldviews was brought home even more to me when, as a transplanted Englishman, I read the Federalist Papers for the first time and realized the sharp contrast between this optimistic view and what I saw as a far more skeptical and realistic view expressed by the Founders. It occurred to me, at that time, that not only was the worldview of many public administration writers quite different from mine, but that it also seemed in conflict with the basic worldview underlying American constitutional governance.

What I have sought to do here, therefore, is to explore the worldviews of public administration and the Constitution. Specifically, I argue that, whereas many if not most public administration writers exhibit a rationalist worldview that places great faith in the powers of human reason, the Founders held, for the most part, a more anti-rationalist worldview that stresses the limits of reason. This conflict in worldviews, I suggest, makes it difficult for us as public administration writers to argue for the legitimacy of public administration on constitutional grounds. In this book, I also explore an alternative vision of public administration—one that I believe is more consistent with the Founders' worldview. Rather than trying to fit the Constitution to public administration, as some writers have done, I have attempted here to fit public administration to the Constitution.

A word or two here is perhaps appropriate on my use of the term "anti-rationalist" to characterize the worldview of the Founders, since, despite my attempts to define it carefully in the text, the term may still convey a misleading impression to some. I have used this term to capture a certain skeptical attitude regarding the powers of reason, but not to imply a rejection per se of reason or any kind of embrace of irrationalism or mysticism. My own arguments here are, after all, an exercise in the use of reason. Aware of possible confusion between anti-rationalism and irrationalism, I had seriously considered using other terms such as "classical liberal" or "conservative" to better capture the idea of this worldview, but concluded that the use of these terms would probably have made my arguments equally, if not more, prone to misinterpretation. I stand, therefore, by my use of the term "anti-rationalist," but ask that the reader take care to understand what I mean and do not mean by this.

This book essentially expands upon my argument developed in an article entitled "Public Administration and the Constitution: A Conflict in World-Views," which was published in the *American Review of Public Administration* (March 1994: 85–95). It also draws ideas from an article, coauthored with my colleague, Larry Terry, entitled "Legitimacy, History and Logic: Public Administration and the Constitution, *"Public Administration Review,* (May/June 1993: 239–246). In this article, we sought, among other things, to examine the logic of the Founders' argument for checking power and its implications for public administration. I would like to thank the American Society for Public Administration here for its permission to reprint some limited material from this article in the book. Thanks are also due to Sage Publications for its permission to reprint small amounts of material from my two articles, "A Contractarian Approach to Public Administration" (*Administration and Society,* November 1990: 303–316) and "On Friedrich Hayek and Public Administration" (*Administration and Society,* May 1993: 46–59). The former work is an attempt to use public choice economics to examine normatively the role of public administration and provides in many ways the genesis for the ideas expressed in this book. The latter work is an attempt to examine the implications for public administration of the work of the late Friedrich Hayek, to whom I owe considerable intellectual debts, as will become apparent to readers as they encounter my arguments.

Other debts are also gratefully acknowledged here. Thanks are due specifically to my colleagues at Cleveland State University, Larry Terry, Lawrence Keller, and William Bowen, lively conversations with whom did much to help the progress of this book. Also, I would like to thank Guy Adams of the University of Missouri at Columbia for his helpful and encouraging comments on many of the key ideas contained in this work. I also thank my Dean, David Sweet, for providing me with the extra time needed to complete this book. Finally, thanks are especially due to my wife, Claudia, whose loving patience and encouragement made this work possible and who, drawing on her skills as a professional librarian, helped me prepare the index for the book. Any remaining errors or flaws in this work are, of course, solely my responsibility.

The Founders, the Constitution, and
Public Administration

1
Introduction: The Uneasy
Status of Public Administration

Americans have traditionally viewed public administrators with, at best, ambivalent feelings. Americans have never quite been comfortable with the large and powerful administrative apparatus that Europeans view as necessary and even desirable in a modern democratic state. The very terms "bureaucracy" and "bureaucrat" have almost always brought to mind negative and often conflicting images in American culture. The media, as public administration writer Charles Goodsell (1985) has noted, portrays the bureaucrat "as lazy or snarling, or both . . . as bungling or inhumane, or both" and "the bureaucracy . . . as over-staffed, inflexible, unresponsive, and power-hungry, all at once" (2). This antipathy towards bureaucracy is not simply confined to the popular culture. Goodsell observes that academics from a wide variety of disciplines, including economics, political science, sociology, and organization theory have charged bureaucracy with a variety of crimes including "failure to perform; abuse of political power; and repression of employees, clients, and people in general" (11). Bureaucracy is, as Goodsell puts it, the "splendid hate object" of American culture (11).

Neither has the growth of government since World War II done much to improve the regard in which public administration is held. Terence Mitchell and William Scott (1987) have noted from opinion polls increasing public distrust and lack of confidence in American administrative leadership. They write of "a prolonged waning confidence of the public in its leadership that seems to cut across the major segments of the administrative state" (445). Mitchell and Scott argue that this change in confidence is not simply a generalized discontent with jobs, institutions, or life. "Rather, the leadership elite of the administrative state is in question" (446). This lack of confidence in the administrative state has fueled the growth of "bureaucrat-bashing" in political campaigns in the 1970s, 1980s, and 1990s. Lack of public confidence in public administration is further shown by the uncritical way in which the findings of the Grace Commission and its tales of overpriced hammers, toilet seats, and screws have found their way into the popular culture.

Herbert Kaufman (1981) has, with some justification, characterized the current antipathy toward public administration as a "raging pandemic." He notes that "more and more people are apparently convinced that bureaucracy is whirling out of control and are both infuriated and terrified by the prospect" (1). The history of the modern state has been characterized, in the words of James Freedman (1978), "by an extended sense of crisis" (9). Americans are uneasy about what role public administration ought to play in their constitutional system of government. Public administration, in other words, lacks legitimacy.

THE LACK OF LEGITIMACY OF PUBLIC ADMINISTRATION

By legitimacy here, I do not mean simply legality. Certainly, as Kenneth Warren (1993) argues, the administrative state is legal. The federal courts have never seriously questioned the legality of delegation of authority to administrative agencies by Congress since the 1930s. Legitimacy, however, means more than simply conformity to law. It also means conformity to the broadly accepted principles or rules and customs of a political and social order. In this broader sense, it is not at all obvious that Americans generally believe that the administrative state is legitimate.

We do not seem to know or agree on what it is that we want public administrators to be or do within our system of government. We seem unable to accept, in principle, the notion that an unelected body, apart from the courts, should have the authority to exercise independent discretionary power over others. Public administration is seen, at best, as a necessary evil in carrying out the public demand for services as expressed through its elected representatives and, at worst, as a self-serving obstacle to the effective provision of such services. Unlike our elected officials and our courts, public administrators are not seen as legitimately exercising any independent influence within the process of government. Observers of government recognize and often accept the existence and even the inevitability of independent administrative action, but they rarely defend it or endorse it on normative grounds.

Earlier in our history, public administrators could perhaps draw some legitimacy from their perceived role as experts in matters of public policy and administration. Woodrow Wilson (1955) saw the possibility of a science of administration that would "seek to straighten the paths of government, to make its business less unbusinesslike, to strengthen and purify its organization and to crown its duties with dutifulness" (6). However, the growth of competing sources of policy expertise in think tanks, consulting firms, universities, congressional staffs, and elsewhere has destroyed whatever monopoly of expertise that public administrators have had in this area. As Aaron Wildavsky (1988) pointed out, this has meant that "virtually everything that officials can say based on their expertise can be contradicted with conviction by these analysts" (753). Francis Rourke (1992) similarly argues that "expertise on public policy issues is now commonly seen as flourishing as abundantly in the outside world as it does within government itself" (540).

Furthermore, the contribution of the modern social sciences, upon which many public administrators depend for their expertise, has frankly been disappointing at least to those who have hoped for a more precise science of public policy and administration. Despite the technical sophistication of much social science modeling, attempts by social scientists to emulate both the generality and the precision of the natural sciences have fallen short. Mitchell and Scott (1987) note that the social sciences have not been able to produce "law-like generalizations which would apply to such major issues as policy formulation, decision making, and strategy" (447). Charles Lindblom (1990) argues even more forcibly that there is an "absence of undeniable evidence" in the social sciences and suggests that it is difficult to "identify a single social science finding or idea that is undeniably indispensable to any social task or effort" (136). The social sciences do not seem to have produced any clearly visible or indisputable improvements in the efficacy and efficiency of government. They have not proven able to provide the knowledge required to cure the social ills of poverty, ignorance, crime, violence, and misery or the political ills of corruption, waste, and abuse of power. Indeed, their prescriptions in the minds of many have seemed often to compound these ills. In light of the limitations of the social sciences, it is difficult then for public administrators to seek legitimacy on the basis of expertise.

The lack of legitimacy of public administration has also, in all likelihood, been exacerbated in the past two decades or so by increasingly sharp ideological divisions in American society. Various factions from both the left and right of the political spectrum seem to state their positions in increasingly strident and uncompromising tones. Issues are increasingly defined or framed in non-negotiable terms. Aaron Wildavsky (1988) wrote of an "ideological dissensus within the political spectrum" involving "profound disagreements over equality, democracy, and hence the role of government, disagreements that create conflicting expectations that no conceivable cadre of civil servants can meet" (753). In the field of environmental policy, for example, public administrators are seen depending on one's ideological perspective as environmental zealots or as puppets of industrial and commercial interests. Because of this type of sharp ideological dissensus, it becomes increasingly difficult to define an acceptable role for public administration.

Whatever they do, public administrators cannot win. They are caught in an ideological cross fire in which media discourse often seems to resemble a form of legalized blood sport rather than an open and civil exchange of ideas. In the absence of consensus surrounding the role of government, bureaucracy becomes increasingly seen simply as a tool by which some groups gain benefits and privileges at the expense of others. Many conservatives in the 1980s viewed public administrators as an obstacle to their attempts to increase liberty and to reduce taxation and government regulation, which they believed were wrecking the economy. Many liberals, in contrast, saw public administration as preserving and reinforcing existing social and economic inequities, as perpetuating economic oppression. They blamed it for the failures of their grand schemes to yield hoped-for results. In such a divisive and hostile ideological climate, it is hardly surprising that whatever legitimacy public administration once had should wither on the vine.

WHY WORRY ABOUT LEGITIMACY?

One may reasonably ask why we should worry over this lack of legitimacy of the administrative state. After all, despite all our complaints about bureaucracy, most Americans do not seem ready to give up big government or to support draconian cuts in public spending programs. Indeed, despite publicity over public spending cuts, public spending continues to grow annually by hundreds of billions of dollars. Current political debate over public spending typically centers on how fast it should grow rather than whether or not it should grow. The administrative state seems, therefore, in no immediate danger of running out of resources. As Mitchell and Scott (1987) argue, so long as government goods and services reach most people, citizens "may cynically withhold trust but support the current structure of the administrative state" (451). If all that lack of legitimacy entails is a few bruised bureaucratic egos, then many may see it as little to lose sleep over.

However, there is probably more to lack of legitimacy than simply bruised bureaucratic egos. Lack of administrative legitimacy can have real costs. Firstly, a perception that public administration is not legitimate can reduce the ability of the administrative state to recruit and retain talented young men and women so that the competence and effectiveness of public service suffers. Evidence collected by the National Commission on the Public Service (1989) seems to confirm that the poor public image of government service has hindered the recruitment and retention of personnel. According to a survey of top graduates undertaken by the Commission, "the public service is not perceived as a place where talented people can get ahead" and very few graduates see a federal job as "challenging and intellectually stimulating" (26). Secondly, lack of administrative legitimacy can undermine the morale of public administrators and reduce their productivity. There is evidence, for example, of increased turnover in the federal service that may, in part, be a result of the declining image of public service (National Commission on the Public Service 1989; Rosen 1983). Such turnover means that knowledge and experience within the service is lost so that again competence and effectiveness suffer.

Thirdly, the perceived lack of legitimacy of public administration can encourage political leaders to impose overly restrictive controls on public administrators that hamper their flexibility and raise the costs of providing services to taxpayers. This is not to deny that rules and procedures are necessary to restrain misuse of resources or abuse of power. To the contrary, as I shall argue in this book, they are crucial. Lack of confidence, however, can help breed a heavy-handed type of "micro-management" that stifles effective administrative action and is counterproductive. Finally, lack of administrative legitimacy can contribute to the erosion of public respect for the law, from paying taxes to observing speed limits. For most citizens, public bureaucracy provides their most important, their most immediate, and sometimes their only encounter with government and the law. As a result, their attitudes toward government and law are inevitably colored by attitudes toward public administrators.

A democratic government, while possessing substantial powers of coercion, must rely heavily on the goodwill and voluntary compliance of citizens in carrying out the law. Without such voluntary compliance, we face the prospect of either an ineffective government or an overly intrusive government. Lack of public respect for the law can then both hamper effective government and reduce the liberty available to citizens.

PUBLIC ADMINISTRATION AND THE U.S. CONSTITUTION

In light of the problem of legitimacy for public administration, it is perhaps to be expected that the constitutional bicentennial in the United States has seen a renewed interest in the relationship between constitutional theory and the structure and process of public administration (Stillman 1987). The Founders, perhaps surprisingly, had little to say specifically on the matter of public administration. However, there has been much discussion and informed speculation as to what type of public administration might be implied by their writings, debates, and actions. Various authors, perhaps most notably John Rohr (1986) and his colleagues at the Blacksburg School (Wamsley et al. 1990), have sought legitimacy for the modern administrative state in the expressed views of the Founders. They have argued that an active and energetic administrative state can be justified on the basis of the writings of the Founders.

Rohr (1986) bases his case for the legitimacy of the administrative state on the "great political argument of 1787/1788" between the Federalists and the Anti-federalists (9). Rohr seeks to demonstrate that the blending of executive, legislative, and judicial powers found in many administrative agencies is by no means inconsistent with the Founders' idea of a separation of powers. He notes that the Founders intended a sharing of powers rather than a rigid separation of powers. Rohr further argues that the administrative state legitimately performs a function originally intended for the U.S. Senate. He sees public administration as providing a continuity and stability to American governance and as exercising a balancing role between the different constitutional branches of government. Also, in Rohr's view, the administrative state provides a remedy to the limits on representation provided by the House of Representatives. He notes the broadly representative character of American bureaucracy. As a result, Rohr interprets the Founders' work as empowering modern public administrators to play an independent constitutional role by choosing among their constitutional masters, who may sometimes be in conflict with one another. Rohr concludes by noting that "the administrative state is a plausible expression of the constitutional order envisioned in the great public argument at the time of the founding of the Republic" (181).

David Hart (1989), taking perhaps an even more ambitious and more romantic interpretation, sees the Constitution as promoting an ethos of "civic humanism," based on love of others. He argues that civil servants should take moral leadership in establishing a "partnership in virtue among all citizens." Hart argues that the Founders' writings can be taken as a basis for obliging public administrators to "form and express independent moral (and technical judgements) about the work they do" and for encouraging them "to exercise discernment, rather than a routine application of rules" (103). He believes that the Founders' work implies an obligation for public administrators "to persuade both citizens and colleagues to do the right" and to act themselves as exemplars of civic virtue and courage (103).

These types of attempts to legitimate a substantial constitutional role for public administration in terms of the thought of the Founders are understandable. As Irving Kristol (1987) has suggested, the U.S. Constitution has, along with the flag and Declaration of Independence, acquired an almost sacramental status in the eyes of most citizens. Kristol argues that "there is a spirit of the Constitution, enveloping the text and transforming it into a covenanting document, a pillar of the American civil religion" (5). Similarly, Rohr (1986) states that "the Constitution is more than a legal document: it is covenant as well as contract" (*x*). By seeking to ground public administration in constitutional principles, these authors and others attempt to draw upon the public affection and respect accorded to the Founders' work. To the extent that an active role in governance for public administration can be justified in a convincing fashion by the Constitution, the more likely it is that such a role will be seen as legitimate.

Furthermore, these attempts make a great deal of sense. Attempts to legitimate public administration must draw on rather than ignore the cultural and political history of the nation. It is important that public administration writers should seek legitimacy for American public administration in terms of political values that are characteristically, although by no means exclusively, American. As Rohr (1993) notes, "The case for public administration should run with the grain of the American political culture, not against it" (246). The Constitution helps establish the "rules of the game" by which Americans conduct their public affairs. It is crucial that the role of public administration be defined in a manner that is consistent with those rules if it is to be seen as legitimate. Certainly, a public administration that acts outside of those rules is unlikely to be seen as legitimate.

CRITICS OF THE CONSTITUTION

However, this love affair between writers in public administration and the Constitution has been relatively recent and, even now, is not universally shared. Public administration writers in the early twentieth century were frequently critical of the Constitution, particularly with regard to the separation of powers. Woodrow Wilson (1956), Frank Goodnow (1900), and W. F. Willoughby (1927), for example, all saw the separation of powers as a constitutional defect. They saw it as an obstacle to effective government and administrative action. Indeed, Wilson, influenced by the British scholar Walter Bagehot, even went so far as to favor constitutional reform along the lines of the British parliamentary system. While backing away from this later in his career, Wilson (1956), nonetheless, argued that "the federal government lacks strength because its powers are divided, lacks promptness because its authorities are multiplied, lacks wieldiness because its processes are roundabout, lacks efficiency because its responsibility is indistinct and its action without competent direction" (206).

This hostility of many early public administration scholars to the separation of powers was typical of most progressive writers of this era such as Charles Beard (1941), who suggested that the Constitution was little more than an attempt to protect the economic interests of the propertied classes.

Beard, a political scientist, was himself, interestingly enough, active in the early public administration movement. However, the critical stance of public administration writers toward the Constitution has endured beyond the heady days of the progressive era. Recently, Lynton Caldwell (1976) has suggested that our constitutional heritage may, in fact, be inadequate in light of the contemporary challenges facing government. According to Caldwell, "It has not been excess of power but defect of responsibility that has most threatened the national welfare" (487).

Richard Stillman (1989), perhaps the sharpest of the contemporary critics, argues against the notion that the state must be "chained and immobilized to the ancient verities of the Founding Fathers" and cautions against "clinging to antiquated republican solutions for contemporary governance" (84). Because of the emphasis of the Constitution on the need to check power, Stillman (1991) sees it as promoting a "stateless" polity. He views it as impeding effective government action and unduly restricting our thinking about public administration and its importance to public welfare. According to Stillman (1991), our preference for "statelessness" not only "creates problems for building effective public administration institutions in the United States but imposes serious blinders on our capacity to think realistically about contemporary public administration theory" (40).

Taking perhaps an even more radical tack, Guy Adams and his colleagues (1990) at Evergreen State College are sharply critical of what they see as the Founders' vision of democracy. Echoing Beard, they argue that "the Constitution confirmed an entire social order embracing specific political/economic relations, private/public divisions, power configurations and developmental directions—and simultaneously disallowed others" (222–223). These authors reject the Founders' liberal and procedural notion of democracy. They call for a "full democracy" that would emphasize common needs and give attention to equality of outcomes for citizens. Like earlier writers, Adams and his colleagues believe that constitutional values impede effective administrative action. They note that, because of an excessive emphasis on these values, "responsiveness and accountability have become profoundly problematic, and tendencies of stasis and drift, engendered by the dynamics of interest group politics, have brought into question the very governability of the modern state" (231).

In quite sharp contrast to Rohr and Hart then, many writers in public administration have been quite critical of the Constitution and have seen it as a constraint on the actions of an effective administrative state. What these criticisms suggest is more than mere differences over the details of constitutional design. Rather, they indicate that many public administration writers may in fact view the world quite differently than did the Founders. This idea is lent some credence by the work of Jeffrey Sedgwick (1987) who notes that the progressives, including Woodrow Wilson, disagreed fundamentally with the Founders regarding "the nature of a just and decent political community" (306–307). According to Sedgwick, whereas the Founders saw a political community as founded out of an interplay of "a variety of interests," the progressives saw the public interest as "conceptually distinct from such an accommodation" (306). These disagreements about views of a political community, noted by Sedgwick, are suggestive of a larger conflict in worldviews.

THE IMPORTANCE OF WORLDVIEWS

By a worldview is meant a sense of how the world works, particularly how the world of human action works. Thomas Sowell (1987) refers to this sense of the world as a "pre-analytic cognition" or a vision. Worldviews provide a frame of reference through which individuals interpret or give meaning to human action. They give us an almost instinctive sense of the causal structure of our reality—a "gut feeling" concerning the causes and consequences of human actions. Without some such sense of causal structure, human actions would be seen as simply a collection of random movements without meaning and would be incomprehensible to us. A worldview, in other words, gives meaning to human action.

Worldviews are not simply collections of facts but rather provide the means by which we structure and give meaning to facts. Even a simple object such as a tool, a food, a medicine, or a weapon would lack any meaning for us in the absence of a sense of the causal structure of human action (Hayek 1948). Neither are worldviews the same as theories, although they provide a set of preconceptions from which theories may be derived. As Sowell notes, Karl Marx's theory of communism was not itself a worldview but could not have been developed in the absence of one. Furthermore, worldviews are not based on logic or reasoning. Rather they shape the objects of our reason and the premises which we use in reasoning.

Worldviews are crucial in our interpretation of social and political institutions. Our very sense of what is meant by a constitution, a government, a legislature, a legal system or, for that matter, a public administration can only become coherent in terms of what we see as the purposes and consequences of human action and this derives from our worldview. Of central importance here are our views of the nature of human beings and the role that reason plays in human affairs. Different views about the nature of humanity and the role of reason lead to very different views about causal relationships in the world and hence to differing interpretations of the meaning of institutions.

It follows then that those who seek to use the Founders' work as a basis for legitimating public administration ought to both understand and embrace significant elements of the Founders' worldview. If we ignore or even reject significant elements of the worldview of the Founders, then it is difficult to see how we can use their handiwork to build a convincing case for a significant constitutional role for public administration. Historical interpretation is, after all, based on an act of communication between the past and present, and communication presupposes some sharing of worldviews. If we say that how the Founders saw the way the world works is no longer quite relevant to contemporary discussions of public administration, then the usefulness or relevance of their work in understanding contemporary public administration is far from clear.

If we are to legitimate public administration in terms of the Constitution, it is necessary to examine the worldviews underlying the work of the Founders and that of writers in public administration to see if they are indeed compatible. If, as suggested in this work, they are not, then we face a choice. We can cease trying to use the Constitution as a basis for legitimating public administration and look elsewhere for legitimacy. Alternatively, we can reassess our own view of public administration in light of their worldview. The arguments presented here are by way of an attempt to provide such a reassessment.

THE PURPOSE OF THIS WORK

The purpose of this book is to examine the worldviews underlying public administration and the Constitution. It is also to see how our vision of public administration might be modified so as to render it more compatible with the worldview of the Founders. In the first part of this book, two rather different ways of looking at the world are presented and used as a framework to contrast the existing literature in public administration and the writings of the Founders. It is argued that there is a conflict in worldviews, in that whereas public administration is rooted in a worldview that stresses the powers of reason, the worldview underlying the design of the Constitution stresses the limits of reason. This conflict in worldviews makes clearer the problem that we face in trying to ground a legitimate public administration in the Constitution. It explains why many, if not most, public administration writers, as noted above, have seen the Constitution as a problem for public administration rather than as the basis for its legitimation. It is argued here that providing legitimacy for public administration in the Constitution requires that we recognize explicitly the worldview of the Founders, and then see how this can be squared with an active public administration.

In the second part of this book, an alternative approach to legitimating public administration is developed; an approach more consistent with the worldview of the Founders, which explicitly recognizes the necessity of checking power the Founders so clearly appreciated. The analysis begins with a development and justification of the case for checking the discretionary power of government officials. Following this, existing visions of public administration are discussed and critiqued in light of the case for checking power. Building on this critique, an alternative vision of public administration is presented and discussed in which administrative discretion is argued for as a means of checking the abuse of political power. The implications of this vision for administrative ethics are also explored. Finally, the relevance of this vision of public administration to the modern administrative state is examined and its implications for public administration thought are discussed.

THE RELEVANCE OF THIS WORK

The central argument of this work is that any attempt to establish the legitimacy of public administration on the basis of the Constitution must reflect, to a significant degree, elements of the worldview of the Founders. One may ask what relevance this work has, focusing as it does on the political thought of long-since deceased eighteenth century white male politicians, to strengthening the legitimacy of public administration today. My answer to this question is that if public administration is to be seen as legitimate, scholars in public administration, at least, need to learn to think, talk, and write about public administration in a way that is consistent with the values of government embedded in our constitutional system.

It is possible, of course, that the Founders' values are no longer understood or seen as relevant by our citizenry. If that is the case, then perhaps we need to resolve harder to educate our citizenry in these founding values. Alternatively we should perhaps consider radical constitutional reform in line with our present values. I frankly doubt, however, that this is the case. In the aftermath of Watergate and the Iran-Contra scandal, citizens today seem to share, for example, the Founders' concern with the abuse of political power by public officials, both elected and appointed. Witness, for example, the current demand for term limits on elected officials. While they are sometimes frustrated with gridlock, citizens generally see merit in a political system that checks the abuse of political power.

Obviously, one should not expect that any particular set of academic scribblings on their own can have a significant influence on the perceived legitimacy of public administration in the American constitutional system. This is especially true when they are of an abstract or theoretical character. The best that can be hoped for here is that this work might begin to influence the dialogue among scholars and public officials about what is the appropriate constitutional role of public administration.

Hopefully, if this occurs, this work will lead academics and practitioners to question their own assumptions and their own views about how the world works, and thereby, to begin to think of, write about, and act within public administration in a slightly different light. No matter how practical we profess to be, our opinions and actions in political affairs, as Thomas Sowell suggests, are inevitably shaped by our visions of the way in which the world works. These visions are shaped in an indirect but important way by what our scholars have written. If the tumultuous national and world events of the past two decades show anything, it is that worldviews do matter and that the power of academic scribblings should not perhaps be entirely discounted.

2
Rationalist and
Anti-rationalist Worldviews

Friedrich Hayek (1948) has argued that the history of human thought reveals two very different ways of looking at the world. One view, termed here a "rationalist" view, stresses the powers of human reason while the other, an "anti-rationalist" view, stresses the limits of reason. As Hayek (1948) noted, the rationalist view assumes that reason "is always fully and equally available to all humans and that everything which man achieves is the direct result of, and therefore subject to, the control of individual reason"(8). In contrast, the anti-rationalist view, according to Hayek, "contends that man has achieved what he has in spite of the fact that he is only partly guided by reason, and that his individual reason is very limited and imperfect" (8). Thomas Sowell (1987), similarly, distinguishes between a vision that stresses the capabilities of human beings and a vision that stresses their limitations. These visions, according to Sowell, entail "different conceptions of how much a given individual can know and understand" (49).

This difference between rationalist and anti-rationalist worldviews or visions is important because our views on the ability of human beings to use reason inevitably shape our views about human relationships, the nature of knowledge, and how we should govern ourselves. The contrast in worldviews, as Hayek (1948) notes, "permeates all social thought" (11). Rationalist and anti-rationalist worldviews lead to radically different visions of what is or what is not a desirable social and political order. The differing emphasis that each of us places on rationalist and anti-rationalist worldviews profoundly affects how we look at questions of government and public policy (Sowell 1987).

Of course, few of us are pure rationalists or anti-rationalists. Most of us combine, consciously and unconsciously, elements of both worldviews in our thinking. Nonetheless, this difference in worldviews is real. As Sowell (1987) suggests, it helps explain "how often the same people line up on opposite sides of different issues" (13). More importantly for purposes of this work, it helps explain the uneasiness of many public administration writers with the principles underlying the Constitution. In order to see this more clearly, it is important to further outline the characteristics of the rationalist and anti-rationalist worldviews and then relate them to public administration and the Founders.

THE RATIONALIST WORLDVIEW

The rationalist worldview sees men and women, potentially at least, as possessing substantial powers of reason and able to use that reason intentionally to improve outcomes for humanity. The rationalist worldview is reflected in Michael Oakeshott's (1991) characterization of a rationalist as one who "believes that unhindered human 'reason' (if only it can be brought to bear) is an infallible guide in political activity" (8). Human problems of misery, poverty, and violence arise, according to rationalists, because of our collective failure to properly exercise our reason. The key to economic, political, and social improvement for the rationalist is the conscious application of human reason. Reason can and should be used to provide the basis for a blueprint for a better human order.

The rationalist is optimistic about the possibility of cooperation on common goals between individuals. Once all are properly informed and educated as to the nature of the common good and the means necessary to achieve it, agreement on action for the collective good becomes possible. Conflict for the rationalist is not inevitable and can be resolved when all individuals realize and honestly and freely commit themselves to what reason demonstrates clearly has to be done. Disagreements flow not from differences in values but from a lack of understanding that can and should be remedied through appropriate leadership, education, and discussion.

For rationalists, there is such a thing as a common good or a common will for a community or a society. The common good is real, and it can be found through the exercise of reason and goodwill. It can further be realized through government as the chief agency of social cooperation within a community. Rationalists place little faith in decentralized or spontaneous forms of human cooperation, such as markets, common law, or cultural norms and rules to advance human progress. They express disdain for any notion of an "invisible hand" in human affairs. From the rationalist perspective, only those institutions that can be consciously designed and controlled through the application of collective reason can really be expected to substantially promote the common good. Rationalists see government as the major instrument by which reason may be applied to human affairs for the enhancement of the common good. From the rationalist perspective, government is an institution driven by common purposes. It is the embodiment of the collective will and reason.

Rationalists distrust ideas derived from customs and traditions. Customs and traditions, unless they can be explicitly linked to collective purposes, are seen as impediments to obtaining true knowledge and must be swept aside. They serve, from a rationalist perspective, only to protect the status quo and the power and prestige of privileged groups or classes in society. Customs and traditions are seen as, only too often, obstacles to securing effective collective action; as excuses for not doing what reason clearly shows must be done.

In contrast, rationalists have a deep faith in the potential of science to aid in our understanding not only of the laws of physical phenomena but also of laws of human behavior and relations. Once these laws of human behavior and social order are properly understood, positive control of human affairs is possible. Human institutions and even human nature are often seen by rationalists as perfectible through the application of science. Moral questions are seen as amenable to scientific inquiry and even resolution. There is also a faith in the power of education to mold the character of humanity and to free it from error and prejudice. The state in this sense is not only reformist but also therapeutic in that it seeks to modify and improve the character or nature of human beings.

Not surprisingly, in light of their faith in science, rationalists tend to view experts as important here. These include experts within academia, public bureaucracy, and industry. Experts, whether in the natural or social sciences, play a key role for rationalists in gaining necessary knowledge for the rational direction of human affairs. Experts also serve an important role in educating the community and in providing necessary informed leadership and guidance. From the rationalist perspective, the community can, through cooperative action aided by scientific expertise, consciously design improved political, economic, and social systems and pursue policies that improve the human condition.

RATIONALIST THOUGHT

As the reader may have observed, the term "rationalism" is used somewhat differently here than it is in philosophy, where it typically is seen as a philosophical outlook "which stresses the powers of a priori reason to grasp substantial truths about the world" (Williams 1967, 69). The type of rationalism discussed here includes not only those writers who emphasize a priori reasoning but also positivists, utilitarians, pragmatists, and even idealists. As such, rationalism would encompass thinking from such diverse political philosophers as Jean-Jacques Rousseau, Antoine-Nicolas de Condorcet, G. W. Hegel, Auguste Comte, John Stuart Mill, and John Dewey. As students of philosophy would remind us, there are, of course, important differences between these authors in terms of epistemology. However, what is common to them is their faith in the power, or at least the potential power, of reason to order human affairs.

A belief in the power of reason aided by goodwill is perhaps best reflected in Rousseau's notion of the general will. For Rousseau, the general will is the will for the common good, the personification of the state at its best. According to Rousseau (1987), "the general will is always right" and it "always tends toward the public utility" (155). Furthermore, "only the general will can direct the forces of the state according to the purpose for which it was instituted, which is the common good" (153). Rousseau's vision of the state was clearly rationalist. The state, for Rousseau is "a moral person whose life consists in the union of its members" (156). It must have a "universal compulsory force to move and arrange each part in the manner best suited to the whole" and "an absolute power over all its members . . . directed by the general will" (156). Rousseau's rationalism is further reflected in his optimism about the ability of individuals to cooperate through government for the common good. He noted that:

> So long as several men together consider themselves to be a single body, they have but a single will, which is concerned with their common preservation and the general well-being. Then all the energies of the state are vigorous and simple, its maxims are clear and luminous, there are no entangled, contradictory interests; the common good is clearly apparent everywhere, demanding only good sense in order to be perceived (203).

Rousseau believed that men and women could be taught to act according to the general will through the power of public education. He believed that the state could and should mold human character. Public education was, for Rousseau (1987), "the state's most important business" (126). By means of public education, children would be "imbued with the laws of the state and the maxims of the general will" (125) and thus would learn "to cherish one another as brothers" and "never to want anything but what the society wants" (126). In light of this optimism about the perfectibility of humankind, it is perhaps not surprising that Rousseau continues to serve as an inspiration for rationalist thinkers.

Rousseau departed from the rationalist worldview only in regard to his skepticism about science. Antoine-Nicholas de Condorcet, in contrast, expressed no such skepticism. His faith in science is shown in his assertion that "without doubt it is only by meditation, which furnishes us with fruitful combinations of ideas, that we can arrive at any general truths in the science of man" (Condorcet 1955, 11). According to Condorcet such a science was needed "for predicting the progress of the human race" and for "directing and hastening it" (11).

Condorcet believed that the important political and moral questions that concern men and women were subject to resolution through reason and science, and that both human beings and institutions could and would be perfected in this fashion. He wrote that "the perfectibility of man is truly indefinite" (Condorcet 1955, 4) and that "the perfection of laws and public institutions, consequent upon the progress of those sciences" would lead to "the reconciliation, the identification of the interests of each with the interests of all" (192). Through science, Condorcet saw the human race in the future as "emancipated from its shackles, released from the empire of fate and from that of the enemies of its progress, advancing with a firm and sure step along the path of truth, virtue and happiness" (201).

Hegel, despite the almost mystical nature of his writing, professed a similar faith in the powers of reason and science. He believed that human history consisted of a growing consciousness of the laws governing physical and social phenomena. The state, in Hegel's view, was the embodiment of this consciousness of universal reason. The state represented the identity of personal will with a true universal will based on reason. According to Hegel (1952), "The state is absolutely rational inasmuch as it is the actuality of the substantial will" (155). Hegel (1947) argued that "when the subjective will of man submits to laws—the contradiction between Liberty and Necessity vanishes" and "the objective and subjective wills are then reconciled" (439). While clearly critical of empirical scientific methods, Hegel, like Condorcet, displayed considerable faith in the general power of science. He believed that "the question of what constitutes the State is one of advanced science, and not of popular decision" (Hegel 1947, 443) and that "the highest point in the development of a people is this—to have gained a conception of its life and condition—to have reduced its laws, its ideas of justice and morality to a science" (1947, 480).

Such faith in reason and science is also evident in Auguste Comte's positive philosophy of science. Comte believed that through a scientific examination of the different stages of history, one could develop laws by which a social and political order should be constructed. Problems of social and political order were, for Comte, merely a result of intellectual anarchy. They could be resolved through the application of science. Even differences in political opinion could and would be resolved by science. Indeed, freedom of conscience and speech, in Comte's view (1974), while "indispensable and salutary" in breaking down the old political order would be destructive in his new order (409). Such freedom, according to Comte, "constitutes an obstacle to reorganization" (409) and leads to the "perpetual aggravation of the intellectual anarchy" (410).

Comte (1974) argued that his positive philosophy "offers the only solid basis for that Social Reorganization which must succeed the critical condition in which the most civilized nations are now living" (36). Consistent with a rationalist worldview, he believed that "whatever is now systemized must be destroyed" and that the pursuit of this philosophy would lead "to the social system which is most suitable to the nature of Man" (836). Through the application of science, Comte, like Condorcet, believed that human nature was subject to perfectibility. Positive morality, according to Comte, "will tend more and more to exhibit the happiness of the individual as depending on the complete expansion of benevolent acts and sympathetic emotions towards the whole of our race" (833). Comte saw experts as playing a central role in his new order. His vision was to be fulfilled by "the cooperation of the best minds in each nation" who would form "a positive Council" (Comte 1974, 787). These thinkers would act by "reviewing and renovating all human conceptions . . . by regulating the application of the system through unremitting instructions of all kinds, and even by philosophical intervention in the political conflicts which must arise till the old social action is exhausted" (787).

John Stuart Mill, while best known as a defender of individual liberty and representative government, nonetheless evoked a similarly rationalist and utopian tone in his writings. Mill (1972) argued that "All the grand sources . . . of human suffering are in a great degree, many of them almost entirely, conquerable by human care and effort" (16). He saw the "present wretched education" and "wretched social arrangements" as "the only real hindrances" to securing general happiness for almost all individuals (13). Mill was critical of the "despotism of custom" and saw it as "everywhere the standing hindrance to human advancement" (138). For Mill, the guide to successful individual and social action was the conscious maximization of utility; the greatest happiness principle. In discussing the means of enforcement of his utilitarian morality, he saw in civilization the strengthening of social ties that would lead the individual "to identify his feelings more and more" with the good of others (33) and generate "a feeling of unity with all the rest" (34). He believed this to be "the ultimate sanction for the Happiness morality" (34).

Mill (1972) was keenly aware of the despotic potential of Comte's positivist philosophy, but, nonetheless, argued that it showed "the possibility of giving to the service of humanity, even without the aid of belief in a Providence, both the physical power and social efficacy of a religion" (34). "By its aid," Mill (1988) argued, "we may hereafter succeed not only in looking far forward into the future history of the human race, but in determining what artificial means may be used . . . to accelerate the natural progress in so far as it is beneficial; to compensate for whatever may be its inherent inconveniences or disadvantages, and to guard against the dangers or accidents to which our species is exposed from the necessary incidents of its progression" (118). Mill (1988) looked forward to the time when "no important branch of human affairs will any longer be abandoned to empiricism and unscientific surmise" and to the completion of "the circle of human knowledge" (119).

John Dewey's language was perhaps less utopian than that of either Comte or Mill, but he too shared their belief that the powers of intellect and science should govern the economic and social order. Dewey (1935) argued for a "dependence upon organized intelligence as the method for directing social change" (87). According to Dewey (1935), "the method of intelligence and experimental control" should be "the rule in social relations and social direction" (92). He believed in a "potential alliance between scientific and democratic method and the need of consummating this potentiality in the techniques of legislation and administration" (Dewey 1939, 101–102).

Dewey was critical of laissez-faire economics and what he saw as classical liberal opposition to government intervention. He saw a need for the increased involvement of the state in society and called for the "social control of economic forces in the interests of the great mass of individuals" (Dewey 1935, 34). Dewey (1947) felt that the classical liberal definition of freedom as freedom from government coercion was far too narrow and argued that "freedom is unreal which does not have at its basis an economic command of environment" (468). In Dewey's (1947) view, the road to true freedom "may be found in that knowledge of facts which enables us to employ them in connection with desires and aims" (466). Dewey also believed that science rather than religion or philosophy could provide a positive basis for moral behavior. He argued that "the social forces effective in shaping actual morality work blindly and unsatisfactorily" (1947, 477) and that "substantial bettering of social relations waits upon the growth of a scientific social psychology" (1947, 479). Dewey's thought is especially relevant to this inquiry since he wrote at a time when public administration was emerging as a field of scholarship.

The writers cited here are merely representative of a broad train of thought which arguably goes back to Plato and includes many others such as Sir Francis Bacon, René Descartes, Henri de Saint-Simon and Karl Marx. In citing the work of the writers above, it is not my intent to engage in an intellectual history of this type of rationalist thought. Such histories have been undertaken both in more breadth and depth and with more elegance elsewhere (Hayek 1979a; Popper 1966a, 1966b). My purpose here is simply to provide some of the flavor of this thought and to illustrate both its pervasiveness and its longevity. Rationalism has historically exerted and continues to exert considerable power over human thought.

What rationalism presents is a profoundly optimistic view of man and his ability to use his reason to exercise control over not only his physical environment but also his social environment. There is a visionary quality in the writings of rationalists that has inspired a variety of political and intellectual movements including progressivism, socialism, communism, and national socialism. However, the influence of rationalism runs much deeper than this. The industrial revolution and the burgeoning of science and technology made rationalism a very modern, a very twentieth century worldview. Despite the totalitarian impulses that it often encouraged, it can also be a liberating view in that it provides a sense for individuals of mastery over what often seem arbitrary, impersonal, repressive, and unfair social forces. While many of us may recoil from its excesses, practically none of us are untouched by this worldview.

THE ANTI-RATIONALIST WORLDVIEW

An alternative worldview, while by no means ruling out a role for reason, sees the powers of human reason in human affairs as inherently limited and inevitably prone to both error and abuse. This anti-rationalist worldview was expressed perhaps more explicitly in the eighteenth century than it is today. According to this view, men and women do not and never can have all of the knowledge or wisdom required to consciously design and run a social order. The anti-rationalist view sees the world, particularly the world of human affairs, as simply too complex and hence too unpredictable for any one mind, however wise, to comprehend and control. Human beings may be able to exercise a modicum of reason in dealing with their own limited private affairs and those of their families, friends, and colleagues. They cannot, however, according to the anti-rationalist view, be expected to extend these powers of reason to the infinitely more complex matters of a community or society comprising thousands and even millions of other unknown individuals and their dealings.

The anti-rationalist sees men and women as fallible creatures. Their behavior, as a rule, is not driven by any reasoned common purposes, but by their passions and selfish interests. As a result, it is unrealistic from an anti-rationalist perspective to expect cooperation between individuals on a wide range of human affairs. Conflicting interests and passions rather than cooper-

ation among individuals are the expected norm for human affairs. Anti-rationalists believe that the preservation of the positive and productive aspects of
human interaction requires that the destructive impulses of individuals be
restrained.

However, they believe that in order to restrain their destructive impulses, individuals cannot rely on their reason alone. Rather, they must rely
on customs and laws that have been developed on the basis of human experience and tradition. These informal and formal rules of conduct structure and
constrain human action so that conflicting interests and passions do not destroy the economic, political, and social order. Government here plays a key
role in enforcing rules that limit human conflict. However, anti-rationalists
see government potentially as an instrument not so much of reason, but
rather of individual and group passions and interests. Therefore, while government is needed to restrain social conflict by enforcing rules of human conduct, government must itself be restrained by rules.

Because of the flawed nature of humanity, anti-rationalists are skeptical
about attempts to design social orders anew on the basis of abstract scientific
principles or scientific experiment. They fear that such efforts will inevitably
have both unforeseen and possibly dangerous consequences. Because of the
inherent limits of human knowledge, experts are not seen as particularly helpful here and may even be dangerous because of their narrow vision of what
constitutes knowledge. Here, the improvement of the condition of humanity
is generally based not on the conscious or intentional application of reason,
but rather on the evolutionary development of rules that govern social interactions. These rules serve not to achieve any concrete or specific agreed upon
objectives or interests. They serve rather to limit the harm that individuals
can do to each other as they pursue their own objectives and interests. Anti-
rationalists do not think it beyond the scope of individuals to use reason to
understand the logic and necessity of such rules and even to make useful
modifications of rules. However, they believe that adherence to rules must be
based on moral sentiments and habit rather than on reason, and that modifications should be undertaken cautiously and be based on tradition and experience rather than on abstract principles.

ANTI-RATIONALIST THOUGHT

This anti-rationalist view is evident in the writings of such authors as John
Locke, David Hume, Adam Ferguson, Adam Smith, and Edmund Burke.
Locke's (1939a) assertion that "the comprehension of our understandings
comes exceedingly short of the vast extent of things" and that "it may be of

use to prevail with the busy mind of man to be more cautious in meddling with things exceeding its comprehension" is consistent with the anti-rationalist view (245). The anti-rationalist view on the limits of reason is also reflected in David Hume's (1987) claim that philosophers "are led astray, not only by the narrowness of their understandings, but by that also of their passions" (160). Hume had only modest expectations regarding human nature and believed that rules were necessary to curb human passions and interests. He argued that "the frailty and perverseness of our nature" make it "impossible to keep men, faithfully and unerringly, in the paths of justice" and that the duty of obedience "must be invented to support that of justice" (38).

Furthermore, according to Hume (1987), although the allegiance to justice is "founded on obvious principles of human nature, it cannot be expected that men should beforehand be able to discover them, or foresee their operation" (39). Hume was skeptical concerning the power of reason in developing political institutions. He argued that "to balance a large state or society, whether monarchical or republican, is a work of so great difficulty, that no human genius, however comprehensive, is able, by the mere dint of reason and reflection, to effect it" (124). Hume believed in the importance of custom and tradition and argued that "a wise magistrate . . . though he may attempt some improvements for the public good, yet will he adjust his innovations, as much as possible, to the ancient fabric, and preserve entire the chief pillars of society and supports of the constitution" (512–513).

Adam Ferguson (1980), a contemporary and colleague of David Hume, was similarly aware of the limits of human reason in designing a political and social order when he argued that "nations stumble upon establishments, which are indeed the result of human action, but not the execution of any human design" (122). Ferguson was critical of those who interpreted history in terms of the rational designs of particular individuals and he argued that "men . . . are wedded to their institutions" and "cannot break loose from the trammels of custom" (123). He saw human progress as essentially evolutionary in character and not the product of a coordinated exercise of reason. Ferguson believed that:

> the establishments of men . . . arose from successive improvements that were made, without any sense of their general effect; and they bring human affairs to a state of complication, which the greatest reach of capacity with which human nature was ever adorned, could not have projected; nor even when the whole is carried into execution, can it be comprehended in its full extent (182).

Also, while Ferguson viewed human beings by nature as both sociable and capable of benevolence, his view of human nature was, nonetheless, distinctly anti-rationalist in character. He argued that "if not restrained by the laws of civil society," human beings would enter "on a scene of violence or meanness, which would exhibit our species, by turns, under an aspect more terrible and odious, or more vile and contemptible, than that of any animal which inherits the earth" (Ferguson 1980, 12). He believed that conflict was endemic to human nature and argued that mankind "find in their condition the sources of variance and dissension; they appear to have in their minds the seeds of animosity, and to embrace the occasions of mutual opposition, with alacrity and pleasure" (20).

Adam Smith, a student of Ferguson, took a similarly anti-rationalist view of human nature. Smith (1982) wrote of "the selfish and original passions of human nature" (135). He argued that "man has almost constant occasion for the help of his brethren" but that "it is vain to expect it from their benevolence only" (Smith 1937, 14). Rather he must "interest their self-love in his favour, and shew them that it is for their own advantage to do for him what he requires of them" (1937, 14). Contrary to current impressions, Smith was neither oblivious nor unsympathetic to the notion that human beings could act out of a concern for the common good. However, Smith also saw a potential dark side to public-spirited behavior. He argued that "a certain spirit of system," which is "apt to mix itself with that public spirit which is founded on the love of humanity . . . often inflames it even to the madness of fanaticism" (1982, 232). Smith (1982) suggested that "the man whose public spirit is prompted altogether by humanity and benevolence" should "respect the established powers and privileges" and should accommodate "his public arrangements to the confirmed habits and prejudices of the people" (233). He was critical of the "man of system" who "is apt to be very wise in his own conceit" (1982, 233). In regard to such a man, Smith (1982) went on to argue that:

He seems to imagine that he can arrange the different members of a great society with as much ease as the hand arranges the different pieces upon a chess-board. He does not consider . . . that in the great chess-board of human society, every single piece has a principle of motion of its own, altogether different from that which the legislature might chuse to impress upon it. If those two principles coincide and act in the same direction, the game of human society will go on easily and harmoniously, and is very likely to be happy and successful. If they are opposite or different, the game will go on miserably, and the society must be at all times in the highest degree of disorder (234).

Finally, Edmund Burke was perhaps the most outspoken and eloquent of anti-rationalists. Burke (1992) saw a "radical infirmity in all human contrivances" (15) and emphasized the "want of foresight in our designs" (16). He further noted that "nothing universal can be rationally affirmed on any moral, or any political subject" (1992, 91). A leading critic of the French Revolution and supporter of the unwritten British Constitution, Burke was skeptical of the powers of reason and convinced of the importance of experience and tradition in political designs. Burke (1955) believed that "we have made no discoveries, and . . . that no discoveries are to be made, in morality, nor many in the great principles of government, nor in the ideas of liberty, which were understood long before we were born" (97). He further suggested that "we are afraid to put men to live and trade each on his private stock of reason, because we suspect that this stock in each man is small, and that individuals would do better to avail themselves of the general bank and capital of nations and of ages" (1955, 99). Burke (1955) was opposed to radical or wholesale reform and argued that a man could not "consider his country as nothing but carte blanche—upon which he may scribble whatever he pleases" but rather should consider "how he shall make the most of the existing materials of his country" (181).

The anti-rationalists then present a much more skeptical and constrained view of men and women and their ability to control their environment. It is a view that seems often to place humanity at the mercy of forces that it can barely comprehend, let alone control. While its pessimistic eighteenth century tone, when stated as explicitly as above, often may seem old-fashioned and unenlightened to some modern minds, it nonetheless continues to strongly influence our thinking, particularly in the English-speaking world. It is the basis for the lack of trust in government endemic to the American character and the basis for the love of tradition endemic to the British character. The anti-rationalist worldview continues to be fueled by the horrors of totalitarianism, the failures of socialism, and the loss of confidence in modern democratic systems. It is the source of our frequent desire simply to be left alone by modern institutions and their experts and officials. It is also the source of our faith that society is better off if we leave individuals to fulfill their desires and ambitions provided that they do not inflict harm on others.

SUMMARY

Clearly, rationalists and anti-rationalists then see the world quite differently in terms of the potential role that reason can play in human affairs. Rationalists have a profound faith in the powers of reason and science, a distrust of custom and tradition, and see the common good as emerging from cooperation on common ends. Anti-rationalists, in contrast, stress the limits of reason and the need for rules and customs, derived from experience, to prevent the conflicting passions and interests of fallible human beings from destroying the social order. It should be noted that most of us obviously do not acquire our worldviews by directly consulting the works of particular philosophers. To the contrary, we receive these views many times removed and internalize them, often quite unconsciously.

The attentive reader may wonder why I have devoted so much attention here to elaborating these visions and recounting the thoughts of political philosophers, long-since deceased. It is because I believe that in our thinking, reading, writing, and acting within public administration, we pay too little attention to the power of the visions that shaped their arguments. We typically like to think of ourselves as practical men and women trying to improve the practice of real-world public administration. To the extent that we consciously or unconsciously draw on the ideas of political thinkers, such as those cited here, it is to provide some apparently particular useful insight into that practice.

However, by neglecting the worldviews from which these ideas have emerged, we are often not aware of fundamental conflicts both among the worldviews of the political thinkers we borrow from, and between their worldviews and our own. As a result, we often mix ideas and arguments that are, at their core, in conflict with each other. This is especially true, in my view, in discussions about public administration and the Constitution. The uneasy relationship that public administration writers and practitioners often seem to have had with the Constitution can only be properly understood in the context of a conflict between these worldviews. Furthermore, to the extent that we are to seek a legitimate vision for public administration from the Constitution, we must understand the Constitution and, to understand the Constitution, we must understand our own worldview as writers, teachers, and practitioners of public administration as well as the worldview of the Founders.

3
The Worldviews of Public Administration and the Constitution

As suggested in the last chapter, few of us are pure rationalists or anti-rationalists, and we combine elements of both worldviews in our thinking about public issues. This is unquestionably true both in the case of writers in public administration and in the case of the Founders. However, there does seem to be a clear difference in emphasis between the worldview held by public administration writers and that held by the Founders. Whereas writings of both early and contemporary writers in public administration have generally reflected a more rationalist worldview, the writings of the Founders seem much more a product of an anti-rationalist worldview. Let us examine first the public administration writers.

RATIONALISM AND PUBLIC ADMINISTRATION: THE EARLY WRITERS

Public administration came of age as a discipline during the progressive era of American history. The progressives, of course, were not revolutionaries and included many business leaders among their numbers. Many of them believed in the advancement of business and bureaucratic values rather than the promotion of abstract ideas of social justice. Nonetheless, they were for the most part deeply rationalist in their thinking. They had an essentially collectivist view of society. They saw society either as an integrated machine or as an organism. Collective goals rather than conflicting interests were to be the agenda of government. The progressives shared a belief in the power of reason and science to remake urban society. Political and administrative reform was a means by which government would be made not only more democratic but also more rational. Professional bureaucracy was to provide the expertise necessary here to implement collective goals effectively and efficiently.

As Dwight Waldo (1984), James Stever (1988), Richard Stillman (1991) and others have observed, these progressive ideas shaped the infant discipline of public administration in the late nineteenth and early twentieth centuries. Early public administration writers had a deep faith in the power of reason and its role in human progress. They were profoundly influenced by doctrines of utilitarianism, legal realism, positivism, and pragmatism. These doctrines all emphasized the powers of reason to order human affairs. Woodrow Wilson captured their philosophical outlook best when he argued that "man by using his intellect can remake society, that he can become the creator of a world organized for man's advantage" (Waldo 1984, 18). Public administration was seen by early writers as an instrument of collective intellect or of collective reason. Herman Finer (1925) made explicit the role of the state in the application of reason when he observed that the civil service "acts on the theory that the good of the individual and of society may be discovered by the processes of social reason and action, and be implemented through statutes" (278).

Public administrators shared the progressives' faith in science. If enough data could be collected and properly analyzed, many believed that one could find the "one best way" of administering public services and render public administration more "business-like." Wilson noted that "the object of administrative study is to rescue executive methods from the confusion and costliness of empirical experiment and set them upon foundations laid deep in stable principle" (Wilson 1955, 13). As Waldo (1984) observed in the late 1940s, a "faith in science and the efficacy of scientific method thoroughly permeates our literature on public administration" (21).

This faith in science is evident in Frederick Taylor's scientific management. For Taylor (1985), scientific management was not simply the application of time and motion studies, but also a program for fundamental social reform. It was a means "toward promoting prosperity, toward the diminution of poverty, and the alleviation of suffering" (14). According to Waldo (1984), the advocates of scientific management envisaged the consequences of their efforts as an "entire world run on the principles of scientific management: universal peace between nations, and between social classes, the ultimate in efficiency and in material satisfactions, liberty and equality in their proper portions, general education and enlightenment" (52). "They dreamed of a new world in which physical forces should be harnessed to achieve man's moral purposes" (Waldo 1984, 52–53). It is perhaps no accident here that Lenin, arguably one of the most powerful and influential rationalists of this century, thought "Bolshevist Russia in need of the Taylor system" (Waldo 1984, 53).

Early public administration writers and practitioners enthusiastically embraced the techniques and philosophy of scientific management. Indeed, Waldo (1984) suggests that the scientific management movement and the public administration movement were "related aspects of a common phenomenon: a general movement to extend the methods and the spirit of science to an ever-widening range of man's concerns" and were in some areas "overlapping or indistinguishable" (49). Within public administration, science was seen as the means to identify principles of administration akin to those of the natural order.

Many writers in public administration believed that certain fundamental principles of public administration could be scientifically discovered and, when applied, would secure economy and efficiency in the administration of public affairs. Leonard White (1926), for example, in his classic text on public administration, observed that "we are wholly justified in asserting that a science of management appears to be immediately before us" (15–16). W. F. Willoughby (1927) argued that "there are certain fundamental principles of general application analogous to those characterizing any science which must be observed if the end of administration, efficiency in operation, is to be secured" (ix). According to Willoughby, "these principles are to be determined and their significance made known only by the rigid application of the scientific method to their investigation" (ix). While any scientific investigation of these principles of administration is difficult to find, this did not stop writers from defining them and listing them in texts on public administration. Although taken mostly as an act of faith, they reflected the conviction among early writers that public administration could and would eventually be a science.

Furthermore, many early writers, influenced by German Hegelianism, firmly believed in the reality of a common purpose or will of the community and in the embodiment of this will in the actions of the state. The state, according to Wilson (1889), was the "organ of society, its only potent and universal instrument" (660). While critical of socialist schemes, he believed, nonetheless, that they "have the right end in view: they seek to bring the individual with his special interests, personal to himself, into complete harmony with society with its general interests, common to all" (659). For Frank Goodnow (1900), perhaps the most explicitly Hegelian of early American public administration writers, "the action of the state as a political entity consists either in operations necessary to the expression of its will, or in operations necessary to the execution of that will" (9). Goodnow saw the mission of public administration as the efficient execution of the will of the State. The fundamental problem of the time, in his view, was securing "harmony between the expression and execution of the state will" (23). This could be accomplished only by removing politics from administration.

This belief in the reality of a common will was also evident in the report of the President's Committee on Administrative Management, which was established in 1936 by President Franklin Roosevelt to provide expert recommendations for executive reorganization, and consisted of some of the leading experts of public administration of the time. These included Louis Brownlow, Charles Merriam, and Luther Gulick. According to their 1937 report, the "grand purpose" of executive reorganization was "to make democracy work today in our National Government; that is, to make our Government an up-to-date, efficient, and effective instrument for carrying out the will of the Nation" (Mosher 1976, 116). Norton Long (1949) appears to have been correct then when he observed in the late 1940s that much of administrative thought "operates on the assumption that there must be something akin to Rousseau's 'volonté générale' to which the 'errant volonté de tous' of the bureaus can and should be made to conform" (260).

Consistent also with the rationalist worldview was the movement to strengthen the power of the chief executive over the administrative activities of government. If the common will was real and expressed through the legislative process, then, at least according to the dominant view of the time, it made sense to execute it in the most efficient and effective fashion—that is, through the chief executive of government. Many early writers felt that government should be reorganized along corporate business lines. Administration was to be centralized and integrated under the hierarchical control of a chief executive. The legislature was then to act as a board of directors determining general policy and reviewing reports of executive actions rather than prescribing them in advance.

Willoughby (1927), a major proponent of this view, argued that "a prime requisite of any proper administrative system is that . . . the chief executive shall be given all the duties and powers of a general manager" (36) and that a "system, under which the legislature seeks to control the details of administrative organization and action . . . is radically wrong" (39). According to Willoughby, giving the chief executive full authority over administration would make it "a single, integrated piece of administrative machinery, one in which its several parts, instead of being disjointed and unrelated, will be brought into adjustment with each other and together make a harmonious whole" (51). He argued that the legislature should "give its directions in general terms" and "that the officers charged with their execution" should "furnish it with detailed data regarding their action" (34).

Finally, most early writers in public administration saw an increased role for government and planning as inevitable, and many saw such an increased role as desirable. According to Waldo (1984), their idea of the "Good Life" was a society in which "the range of government control is unquestionably large and the machinery of administration extensive" (68). Waldo suggests that although early students of administration "profess and believe in democracy, liberty and equality, they have generally accepted the alternative of a planned and managed society" (19). Indeed Waldo notes a parallel between the early public administration movement and the British Fabian Socialists (76). Public administration writers saw increased government as a means for introducing both greater rationality and greater fairness in the conduct of human affairs and were generally disdainful of laissez-faire economics. They were optimistic about the ability of government and public administrators to cure the ills afflicting modern industrialized society.

Woodrow Wilson (1955) seemingly embraced this view of government when he argued that "seeing every day new things which the state ought to do, the next thing is to see clearly how it ought to do them" (6). Also, Willoughby (1927) asserted that "the province of government is now held to embrace all forms of activity which contribute in any way to the promotion of public welfare" (*viii*). Similarly, Leonard White (1926) acknowledged "the state as a great agency of social cooperation, as well as an agency of social regulation" and as an "important means by which the program of social amelioration is effected" (8). The President's Committee on Administrative Management clearly also envisaged an extensive role for government when it declared that "we wish to set our affairs in the very best possible order to make the best use of all our national resources" (Mosher 1976, 113). Charles Merriam (1941), a member of that group, perhaps best exemplified this expansive and rationalist view of government when he argued that "planners must consider all the resources of the nation, and strive for the highest and best use by the community" (93).

RATIONALISM AND PUBLIC ADMINISTRATION: CONTEMPORARY WRITERS

With the fragmentation of the field of public administration following World War II (Stever 1988; Stillman 1991), the rationalist view is no longer expressed in quite so clear or evangelical a fashion. Nonetheless, it continues to have a dominant influence in public administration thinking. Herbert Simon (1945) considerably narrowed the scope of rationalism, at least for some, by distinguishing facts from values. Nonetheless, his vision of administration was an essentially rationalist one of an organization rationally designed using empirical science to achieve efficiency. In this sense, the rationalism of Simon and his disciples is perhaps simply more instrumental in character than that of earlier writers.

Some modern public administration writers, inspired by Simon, argue for an interdisciplinary "design science" of public administration that would seek improved designs through interdisciplinary science not only at the task level and the organizational level, but also at the constitutional level. According to this approach, "Good designs are efforts that meet public demand for policy output in an effective and efficient manner" (Shangraw and Crow 1989, 157). The role of public administration as a field "is to design and evaluate institutions, mechanisms, and processes that convert collective will and public resources into social profit" (Shangraw and Crow 1989, 156). While these authors claim their intellectual roots in Alexander Hamilton, their vision of public administration is perhaps more reminiscent of Condorcet or Comte.

The strength of the rationalist worldview is also suggested in the work of those who seek a renewed emphasis on research into what has been termed public management. Indeed, the very term "management" as opposed to "administration" is itself more conducive to a rationalist way of thinking. Public management scholars tend to downplay politics. They seek to emphasize the more generic and rationalist aspects of administration. In a thoughtful review of literature in this area, Sam Overman (1984) has noted that its major features include an "instrumental orientation favoring criteria of economy and efficiency" and a "strong philosophical link with the scientific management tradition" (278). John DiIulio (1989), an advocate of this emphasis on public management, suggests that the purpose of this field should be "to search systematically (if not always 'scientifically') for ways to realize public goals by the most appropriate administrative arrangements possible" (131). Using an organismic analogy often typical of rationalism, DiIulio sees public organizations as the "hands and feet" of "important public purposes" (131–132).

Another example of the pervasiveness of the rationalist worldview is to be found in the current popularity of agency theory. Agency theory, based in economics, examines how rational principals develop and monitor contracts with their agents in order to pursue their goals most efficiently. The key problem, according to agency theory, is controlling the behavior of agents so that their actions are consistent with the efficient attainment of the goals of principals. Terry Moe (1984) has suggested the applicability of agency theory to public organizations. Moe argues that:

> Democratic politics is easily viewed in principal-agent terms. Citizens are principals, politicians are their agents. Politicians are principals, bureaucrats are their agents. Bureaucratic superiors are principals, bureaucratic subordinates are their agents (765).

This view of public administration as an agent of the will of citizens and their representatives is fundamentally rationalist. The fact that agency theory has even found its way into the work of writers such as Henry Kass (1990) and Gary Wamsley (1990), neither of whom are generally associated with the instrumental rationalism that undergirds it, is perhaps illustrative of the pervasiveness of the rationalist way of looking at public administration.

Similarly, the preoccupation of writers since the 1960s with more rational systems of budgeting (Schick 1966) designed to enhance government planning reflects a clearly rationalist view of the world. Also, the growing emphasis on policy analysis, management science, and systems analysis in public administration in the 1960s and 1970s, the current focus on computers and management information systems, and the current popularity of "strategic planning," "total quality management," and techniques for "reinventing government" provide evidence of a continuing faith in rationalism and science. It is true that both political scientists, such as Aaron Wildavsky (1979), and organization theorists such as Robert Golembiewski (1992), have noted the problems that human factors present for rational government designs. However, their purpose is often to simply expand the range of factors that must be taken into account in rational action. This is perhaps most clearly evidenced in the recently published *Handbook of Public Administration* (Perry, 1989), a compilation of contributions from a variety of disciplinary perspectives, which advertises itself both as a "how to" and a "how do we know it" book, "intended to help public administrators act effectively in accomplishing their delegated missions" (*xiv*).

Even the so-called New Public Administration, despite its critiques of mainstream science and public administration, contained some clearly rationalist ideas. George Frederickson (1971) makes clear its ambitious and rationalist agenda when he asserts that the "new Public Administration seeks to change those policies and structures that systematically inhibit social equity" (312). He shares the rationalist faith in science when he envisages "quantitatively inclined public-organization theorists . . . executing a model or paradigm of social equity" that might make it possible "to assess rather precisely the likely outcomes of alternative policies in terms of whether or not the alternative does or does not enhance equity" (330). More recently, Frederickson (1990) argues for the need for a "fully developed compound theory of equity" that "must define, if not predict, the effects of alternative policies, organizational structures, and management styles on the equity of public programs" (235–236).

Similarly, while several current writers, drawing on interpretivism and critical theory, are critical of rationalism, their critique seems often to focus on the instrumental nature and neutral character of rationalism in public administration rather than rationalism per se. Robert Denhart (1981), for example, argues that "truly rational action can occur only by removing restrictions on communications" (631) and that through "a process of generalized critical self-reflection, we may restore the intimacy of theory and practice needed for enlightened human action" (632). Jay White (1990) similarly advocates a "practical discourse" among public decision makers, informed by interpretive and critical reasoning, about the "rightness of the ends to be sought and the means to achieve them" (143). Bayard Catron and Michael Harmon (1981) also take a distinctly rationalist tack when they suggest that public administration theorists should assist public administrators by, among other things, "determining the extent to which the exercise of formal (hierarchical) authority helps or hinders the creation and transmission of shared meanings that enable cooperative, responsible action," and by "engaging both internally and with relevant parties in its environment, in an ongoing assessment of the organization's overall goals, its methods of dealing with environmental groups, and even its reason for being" (538).

What interpretivists and critical theorists seek to do, in my view, is to broaden the definition of truth and to make us aware of less hierarchical, more creative, and participative approaches to finding truth, but they do not, for the most part, seem to deny its existence or the role of the state in bringing us closer to truth. While, like David Hume and Friedrich Hayek, they emphasize the essential subjectivity of human experience, they also seem to retain a characteristically rationalist faith in the power of participatory collective discourse, guided by critical analysis, which calls more to mind the writings of Rousseau; a faith that men and women, when properly enlightened *Madison,* about their true condition, can put aside their conflicting selfish interests and *Fed #10?* passions and can collectively, through a process of open discourse, seek and find the common good. Denhart (1981) seems to affirm such a faith when he observes that "by engaging in a critique of conditions of excessive domination we may be led to new possibilities for more effective public action, possibilities that present themselves close at hand" (634). Discourse for many of these writers appears then to serve not as a means of seeking compromises among individuals and groups with conflicting interests and passions, as anti-rationalists might argue, but rather as a means of promoting more rational and enlightened thought and action.

Despite the profusion, therefore, of different approaches in public administration, the rationalist worldview would seem to continue to exercise strong influence over the way in which we think and write about public administration. Dwight Waldo (1984), in reviewing the contemporary relevance of early work in public administration, seems to confirm this. He notes that "in four decades, nothing has caused me to change my view of scientific management as a locus of political theory" (*xxxi*). Waldo also argues that, in public administration, "the belief that principles, in the sense of lawful regularities, can be discovered by scientific inquiry remains strong" (*liii*). Furthermore, with reference to the New Public Administration and interpretive and critical theories of public administration, Guy Adams (1992) observes that, although a number of new approaches are "thought of as affording an entirely new view of the field, the old images continue to bleed through . . . images of technique and rationality" (370).

Whether or not this continued influence of rationalism on public administration is desirable per se obviously depends upon the worldview of the reader. My purpose at this point is simply to suggest that the ideas of Rousseau, Condorcet, Comte, Dewey, Hegel, and others have cast a long shadow over public administration, as they have over much of contemporary social science (Lindblom 1990), and that they affect fundamentally the way in which public administration writers view the world. The problem from my perspective is that the worldview taken here would seem to conflict with that taken by the Founders.

ANTI-RATIONALISM AND THE FOUNDERS

The very notion that one could create a constitution anew might strike many at first glance as profoundly rationalist and certainly one can find quotations in the Federalist Papers that suggest such a worldview. Alexander Hamilton, for example, asked rhetorically "whether societies of men are really capable or not, of establishing good government from reflection and choice, or whether they are forever destined to depend, for their political constitutions, on accident and force" (Wills 1982, 2). However, there is, in my view, a much stronger anti-rationalist dimension to the Federalist Papers.

Firstly, as public administration writers such as Woodrow Wilson, Lynton Caldwell, and Richard Stillman have noted, the Constitution and the notion of a separation of powers drew heavily from the British custom and law that formed the British Constitution and that shaped colonial political institutions. Wilson (1889) argued that "the political institutions of the United States are in all their main features simply the political institutions of England, as transplanted by English colonists . . . worked out through a fresh development to new and characteristic forms" (449). According to Caldwell (1976), "the 18th century legacy of colonial political ideas was drawn selectively from an earlier England—from the constitutional disputes of the 17th century Civil war and Commonwealth" and was "reinforced, but also reshaped, during the century-and-a-half of relatively isolated colonial experience" (479). In Stillman's (1991) view, "The U.S. Constitution essentially both revitalized and rearranged old, but dying English Tudor institutional customs of fundamental law and balanced government" (27).

Furthermore, in justifying their designs, the Founders drew extensively on examples from history—from ancient Greece and Rome, from the Renaissance and from Britain. While aware of the limitations of drawing from historical experience, James Madison thought experience "the guide that ought always to be followed, whenever it can be found" (Wills 1982, 267). History for Madison "presents to mankind so many political lessons, both of the monitory and exemplary kind" (287). The constitutional design of the Founders also drew upon and was driven by their more immediate experience with problems arising from the Articles of Confederation, in particular the excesses of state legislatures and the inadequacy of national defense. Their major concern was to design a constitution that would remedy these problems. This reliance for constitutional design on tradition and history modified by experience is more consistent with an anti-rationalist worldview than a rationalist worldview.

Secondly, the Founders were well aware of the limits of reason as applied to constitutional design. Madison, considering these limits, warned that, in understanding human institutions, we must moderate "our expectations and hopes from the efforts of human sagacity" (Wills 1982, 179). Madison noted "the obscurity arising from the complexity of objects, and the imperfection of the human faculties" (179) and the "unavoidable inaccuracy" of the "cloudy medium" of language (180). In discussing the constitutional convention, Madison felt it a wonder "that so many difficulties have been surmounted; and surmounted with a unanimity almost as unprecedented as it must have been unexpected" (181). He, furthermore, warned against frequent constitutional reform because of the "danger of disturbing the public tranquility by interesting too strongly the public passions" (256).

Hamilton's awareness also of the limits of reason is clearly exhibited in his references to "Utopian speculations" (Wills 1982, 21) and to "airy phantoms" that flit before "distempered imaginations" (37). In defending the Founders' constitutional proposals, Hamilton warned against "the chimerical pursuit of a perfect plan" and argued that "the result of the deliberations of all collective bodies must necessarily be a compound as well of the errors and prejudices, as of the good sense and wisdom of the individuals of which they are composed" (446). He suggested that we should "never expect to see a perfect work from imperfect man" (446). Hamilton further asked:

Have we not already seen enough of the fallacy and extravagance of those idle theories which have amused us with promises of an exemption from the imperfections, weaknesses and evils incident to society in every shape? Is it not time to awake from the deceitful dream of a golden age, and to adopt as a practical maxim for the direction of our political conduct, that we, as well as the other inhabitants of the globe, are yet remote from the happy empire of perfect wisdom and perfect virtue (26)?

Finally, and perhaps most importantly, the Constitution emphasized the decidedly anti-rationalist notion of checking political power. The Founders viewed the checking of power as fundamental to their constitutional design. This was why they devised the constitutional institutions of the separation of powers, bicameralism (a separately elected House and Senate), and federalism. Madison's argument for the Union was based on the notion that an extended republic would make it more difficult for various factions in society to use majority rule to exploit citizens. As Madison noted:

Extend the sphere, and you take in a greater variety of parties and interests; you make it less probable that a majority of the whole will have a common motive to invade the rights of other citizens; or if such a common motive exists, it will be more difficult for all who feel it to discover their strength, and to act in unison with each other (Wills 1982, 48).

Madison's argument for a stronger central government is based on its role in checking the abuse of discretionary power by majority factions in state legislatures. According to Madison, "When a majority is included in a faction, the form of popular government . . . enables it to sacrifice to its ruling passion or interest, both the public good and the rights of other citizens" (45). Federalism, by checking the excesses of state legislatures, would provide "a Republican remedy for the diseases most incident to Republican government" (49).

At the same time, Madison also argued for a separation of powers as a means of checking the power of majority interests at the federal level. Separation of powers between the executive, legislative, and judicial branches of government is desirable, according to Madison, because "ambition must be made to counteract ambition" (Wills 1982, 262). Madison's constitution is designed to overcome the "defect of better motives" by providing for "opposite and rival interests" (263). According to Madison, "the constant aim is to

But what was the purpose of the checks?
To regulate interests — menace likelihood
that reason rather [*Anti-rationalism and the Founders* * 37]
than passion would prevail

divide and arrange the several offices in such a manner as that each may be a check on the other" (263).

So convinced was Madison of the need to check power that he believed that a check was necessary within the legislative branch itself; namely, the Senate. According to Madison, legislative assemblies were prone "to yield to the impulse of sudden and violent passions, and to be seduced by factious leaders, into intemperate and pernicious resolutions" (315). A Senate was necessary "as a defence to the people against their own temporary errors and delusions" (320). By means of the Senate, the "interference" of a "temperate and respectable body of citizens" would "check the misguided career" and "suspend the blow mediated by the people against themselves, until reason, justice and truth" could "regain their authority over the public mind" (320).

Hamilton is frequently portrayed, particularly by public administrators, as a proponent of both a strong federal government and a strong executive. His arguments, however, also reflect a concern with the need to check political power. Indeed, Hamilton's argument for a strong executive is based in part upon his assessment of the dangers of unrestrained legislative power. "Energy in the Executive" was for Hamilton essential to "the protection of property against those irregular and high-handed combinations, which sometimes interrupt the ordinary course of justice" and to "the security of liberty against the enterprise and assaults of ambition, of faction and of anarchy" (Wills 1982, 355). Hamilton, in defending the notion of an executive veto, made clear his rationale for checking power:

> It may perhaps be said, that the power of preventing bad laws includes that of preventing good ones; and may be used to the one purpose as well as to the other. But this objection will have little weight with those who can properly estimate the mischiefs of that inconstancy and mutability in the laws, which form the greatest blemish in the character and genius of our governments. They will consider every institution calculated to restrain the excess of law-making, and to keep things in the same state, in which they happen to be at any given period, as much more likely to do good than harm; because it is favorable to a greater stability in the system of legislation. The injury which may possibly be done by defeating a few good laws will be amply compensated by the advantage of preventing a number of bad ones (373–374).

Finally, Hamilton argued for an independent judiciary on the grounds that it would serve as an "excellent barrier to the encroachments and oppressions of the representative body" and would "secure a steady, upright and impartial administration of the laws" (393). He also saw an independent judiciary as necessary "to guard the constitution and the rights of individuals from those ill humours which the arts of designing men, or the influence of particular conjectures, sometimes disseminate among the people themselves" and which "have a tendency . . . to occasion dangerous innovations in the government, and serious oppressions of the minor party in the community" (397).

The Founders felt that checks on power were necessary because they did not trust elected officials to exercise reason in the conduct of public affairs. As Madison noted in his oft-quoted argument:

> If men were angels, no government would be necessary. If angels were to govern men, neither external nor internal controuls on government would be necessary. In framing a government which is to be administered by men over men, the great difficulty lies in this: You must first enable the government to controul the governed; and in the next place, oblige it to controul itself (Wills 1982, 262).

Consistent with the anti-rationalist worldview, the Founders were skeptical of the powers of reason and saw human nature as governed by selfish interests and passions. Hamilton was most explicit in this regard. He observed that "momentary passions and immediate interests have a more active and imperious controul over human conduct than general or remote considerations of policy, utility or justice" (24) and that "the passions of men will not conform to the dictates of reason and justice" (72). Madison argued that "as long as the reason of man continues fallible . . . different opinions will be formed" and that "as long as the connection subsists between his reason and his self-love, his opinions and his passions will have a reciprocal influence on each other" (43). For this reason, the Founders were pessimistic about the possibility of cooperation toward the common good. Madison wrote that "the diversity in the faculties of men . . . is not less than an insuperable object to a uniformity of interests" (43–44) and that the "latent causes of faction are thus sown in the nature of man" (44).

The Federalists' concern with the need to check discretionary power was echoed by the Anti-Federalists. The Anti-Federalists differed with the Federalists in arguing that the Constitution would not provide an adequate check on federal government power, but not with regard to the need to check power. Brutus, in his critique of federal legislative power, warned that "power lodged in the hands of rulers to be used at their discretion, is almost always exercised to the oppression of the people, and the aggrandizement of them-

[handwritten margin note, top:] Madison: not the threat of govt., per se; but majority control of it -- what's discretion got to do with it?

selves" and that "powerful checks" were necessary to prevent the abuse of political power (Ketcham 1986, 331). Similarly, Cato noted that "rulers in all governments will erect an interest separate from the ruled, which will have a tendency to enslave them" (Ketcham 1986, 324).

It is interesting to contrast here the views of the Founders on checking political power with those of rationalists. Checks on the exercise of power are inimicable to rationalism because they constrain the exercise of reason. If individuals are able through reason to agree on the common good, then checks on political power would seem unnecessary and obstructive. Such checks lead, according to a rationalist worldview, to a fragmentation of sovereignty based on the general will. *[handwritten:] What was the purpose of the checks?*

[handwritten margin note:] checks force they began or cut least make it more likely.

Hegel (1952) saw this when he argued that Montesquieu's notion that independent powers should be used to check each other "destroys the unity of the state, and unity is the chief of all desiderata" (292). Condorcet (1955) was also disdainful of the separation of powers and, partly for this reason, thought the American revolution vastly inferior to its French counterpart. He saw constitutions of the American type as "tainted with the prejudices that those who drafted them had imbibed in their youth" and argued that their "simplicity was impaired by the determination to preserve a balance of power within the state" (145). For the utilitarian philosopher Jeremy Bentham (1962), any constitutional limitation on the "omnicompetence" of the legislature was "in contradiction to the greatest happiness principle" (119) and tended "to produce evil to an unlimited degree" (120). These rationalists correctly perceived that checks and balances constrain the exercise of reason and, therefore, could see little if any value in them. A constitutional system of checks and balances can only make sense to those who believe that the power of reason to order human affairs is limited and is then a product of an anti-rationalist worldview.

[handwritten margin note:] no -- encourage it!

CONCLUSION

The academic field of public administration and the Constitution are, therefore, based on very different views of the way in which the world works. Whereas public administration is rooted in rationalism, the Constitution is significantly anti-rationalist in character. This helps explain why public administration writers, as noted earlier, have frequently been critical of the Constitution, particularly with regard to the separation of powers. It also helps explain why even John Rohr, while arguing for a constitutional basis for public administration, is careful to distance himself from the anti-rationalist character of the Constitution.

While by no means a rationalist himself, Rohr (1986) argues nonetheless that too much emphasis has been placed on the Founders' fear of abuse of power and that it is necessary to "neutralize" this aspect of the Founders' argument if "we are to legitimate the administrative state" (7). Rohr's argument concerning the separation of powers is directed toward justifying the exercise of executive, legislative, and judicial power by administrative agencies, and it downplays its fundamental role as a check on political power. Indeed, while he argues that public administration fulfills a role originally intended for the Senate, Rohr does not seem to view this role primarily as one of checking power, noting that "neither a Senate nor a bureaucracy that resists popular whim is a likely candidate for plaudits today" (39).

By downplaying the anti-rationalist character of the Constitution, Rohr and his colleagues make his argument more palatable to a field in which a rationalist worldview is still dominant. However, in doing so, they do not come to grips with the fundamental contradiction in worldviews that separates the Founders of the Constitution from the founders of public administration and their intellectual offspring. As a result, despite their admirable intentions and formidable scholarship, the Constitution is likely to continue to be seen by many, if not most, public administration writers as a problem for public administration rather than as the basis for its legitimation.

Given the continued dominance of a rationalist worldview in public administration thought, grounding public administration in the Constitution will then always be problematic, and the Constitution will always be viewed as a constraint or even a problem. This is unfortunate. As Rohr and his colleagues correctly point out, securing legitimacy for an active administrative state is difficult where public administration is seen in conflict with constitutional principles. If public administration is to be successfully grounded in the Constitution, we need, therefore, to come to terms with the Constitution and the anti-rationalist sentiments of the Founders. This requires a recognition of the relevance of anti-rationalism to public administration thinking and practice.

4
On the Checking of Power: The Logic of a Constitution

If we are to ground public administration in the Constitution, we must recognize explicitly the anti-rationalist character of the Constitution and see how this can be squared with an active public administration. This requires a vision of public administration that incorporates anti-rationalist elements, particularly regarding the idea that <u>political power should be constitutionally checked</u>. The idea of constitutionally checking power, as we have seen, is decidedly anti-rationalist and is explicitly rejected by rationalists. This idea is also an important part of our Anglo-American political tradition. Its incorporation into an anti-rationalist vision of public administration is, therefore, not entirely inappropriate.

However, as has also been made clear in the previous chapters, the constitutional checking of power is not without controversy within public administration. Writers in public administration have tended to be critical of it or have sought to deemphasize it. Therefore, while in no way discounting the importance of political tradition, it may be useful to enlist the aid of reason by examining <u>the logic of a constitution</u>. By the logic of a constitution is meant the reason or reasons why we, as a community of reasonable but fallible human beings, should wish to impose constitutional limits on the discretionary power of government officials. This is admittedly a form of rational analysis, but it is rational analysis directed itself against the excessive claims of rationalism. The question posed here can be restated as asking why we would not wish government officials to exercise unrestrained discretionary power. As such, this analysis follows in the anti-rationalist tradition of David Hume who sought "to whittle down the claims of reason by the use of rational analysis" (Wolin 1954, 1001). It is consistent with Friedrich Hayek's (1960) argument that "a most important and difficult exercise of reason" is "to seek appropriate limits to the uses of reason" (69).

INTERESTS

One reason that we might wish to check the discretionary power of government officials constitutionally is that they are, like us, fallible men and women and can be expected to use their discretionary power on occasion to

41

pursue their own interests, even when it is at our expense. David Hume (1987) captured this idea when he observed that:

> Political writers have established it as a maxim, that, in contriving any system of government, and fixing the several checks and controuls of the constitution, every man ought to be supposed a knave, and to have no other end, in all his actions, than private interest. By this interest we must govern him, and, by means of it, make him, notwithstanding his insatiable avarice and ambition, co-operate to the public good. Without this, say they, we shall in vain boast of the advantages of any constitution, and shall find, in the end, that we have no security for our liberties and possessions, except the good-will of our rulers; that is, we shall have no security at all (42).

According to Hume (1987), if "separate interest be not checked, and be not directed to the public, we ought to look for nothing but faction, disorder and tyranny" (43). Edmund Burke (1968) made a similar point when he argued that a "state which lays its foundation in rare and heroic virtues will be sure to have its superstructure in the basest profligacy and corruption" (294). This argument, as we have seen in the last chapter, was also essentially the one taken by the Founders. The Founders' checks on power were designed to compensate for "the defect of better motives" in government by providing for "opposite and rival interests" (Wills 1982, 263). It has been suggested, of course, that the Founders sought constitutional checks on government power merely to preserve their own social and economic status and power (Beard 1941). However, whatever the motives of the Founders, there is a persuasive logic to their argument.

If we accept that government officials act in their self-interest, then we must recognize that, in the absence of any checks on their discretionary power at all, they will have little if any incentive to take account of the costs that their actions may impose on us. The actions of government, in other words, may impose what economists term negative externalities on us in much the same way that a polluting firm imposes costs upon a surrounding community. This is not to deny, of course, that the actions of government officials may have positive value in providing us with public goods and services, such as law and order, defense, roads, and environmental protection. Nor is it to advocate a laissez-faire state or a night-watchman form of government. Rather, it is simply to point out that, in ceding power to government, we must recognize that government officials may be motivated to use their coercive powers to exploit us. The exploitation of citizens by government officials may take a variety of forms including oppressive taxation, expropriation, discrimination in the provision of government services, and even political violence and murder. Given the potential cost to us of such exploitative actions by self-interested government officials, some checks or limits on the discretionary power of political leaders then would seem necessary.

Constitutions play a central role here in checking the exercise of discretionary power since they determine the "rules of the game" by which public policies are made and implemented. While constitutions may establish institutions of government, their central purpose is to check the exercise of power (Hayek 1979b; Satori 1962). Constitutional rules can limit the discretionary power available to government officials in at least two ways. They can prohibit or block certain actions on the part of government officials, as does, for example, the Bill of Rights, or they can provide particular government institutions with an effective veto power over the actions of other institutions, as does the separation of powers. Whatever their form, constitutional rules can be seen as providing a formal system of checks on the potentially exploitative *purchase* power of government that arises from the self-interested behavior of govern-*behaviors ?* ment officials. As Hume (1987) observed, "the particular checks and controuls" provided by a constitution, if "wisely constituted," should have the effect of making it in the interest, "even of bad men, to act for the public good" (15–16).

This idea that actors in the political process can be expected to pursue their self-interest is basic to economic analyses of the political process undertaken by public choice economists such as James Buchanan (1975). Not surprisingly, these economists also see constitutional checks on power as a necessary means of limiting the costs that government can impose upon citizens. The assumption of self-interest, however, is controversial, at least among some scholars in political science and public administration, where, as York Willbern (1984) has noted, students "have nearly always known that what public officials and employees do has an inescapable normative component, involving values, morality and ethics" (102).

Steven Kelman (1987), for example, has sharply criticized the idea that the public policy-making process can be understood in terms of the self-interest of participants in the process. Kelman argues that whereas people express self-interest in the marketplace, they give "pride of place" to public spirit in their political behavior. He is critical of Madisonian and pluralist theories of government, both of which emphasize the spreading of power and the consequent checking of interests as the major means of promoting good public policy. Kelman claims that the presence of public spirit plays a major role in the policy-making process. In support of his claim, he argues that the growth of

He didn't understand Madison
well enough, either.

government in the 1970s and its limitation in the 1980s are evidence of "the ability of ideas to overcome interests" (Kelman 1987, 248).

Kelman's claim that public-spirited behavior is more common in the public sector than in the private sector would have been disputed by Hume (1987), who observed that "men are generally more honest in their private than in their public capacity" (43). However, even if we concede, as any reasonable individual would, the presence of public-spirited behavior in the public policy process, this does not necessarily undermine the logic of the argument pursued here. Even if government officials were not typically expected to seek their own interests at the expense of citizens, an argument could still be made that a community of reasonable individuals would seek constitutional checks on the discretionary power of government officials.

This is because such checks provide a form of insurance policy for individuals against at least the risk of an exploitative government (Brennan and Buchanan 1985). Government, after all, has the power to destroy both our property and our lives and it may be wise for us, in such circumstances, to exercise a special degree of caution in circumscribing its discretionary powers. Hence, any evaluation of the need to limit or check political power ought to be made on the basis of behavioral assumptions that are perhaps more pessimistic than those we might ordinarily hold on the basis of empirical observation.

In other words, checks on the discretionary power of government officials are necessary not so much to control the type of government that we might hope for, or even expect, but rather to control the type of government that we might fear. Karl Popper (1966a) perhaps articulates this idea best when he notes that "it is reasonable to adopt, in politics, the principle of preparing for the worst, as well as we can, though we should, of course, at the same time try to obtain the best" (122). The assumption of self-interest, as William Eskridge (1988) has argued, "offers a useful way to think about legislation, precisely because it shows the process at its worst" (322). The use of the assumption of self-interest in the argument for checking power can be seen here then as serving as "an excellent warning beacon" (Eskridge 1988, 322); a beacon whose purpose is not so much to predict certain disaster, but rather to remind us of possible danger, in this case, the danger of exploitation of citizens by government officials. Therefore, even if government officials were typically public-spirited, the possibility that they might engage from time to time in self-serving behavior would seem sufficient for us, as a community of reasonable individuals, to justify checks on their discretionary power.

PASSIONS

While the case for using self-interest as an assumption in constitutional discourse is strong, the argument for constitutional checks on power need not, however, rest on self-interest alone. When our interests and values are diverse, as an anti-rationalist perspective would suggest is inevitable in light of the limits of our reason, then conflicting notions among us as to what constitutes the public good will be inevitable. This means that even the presence of public-spiritedness in the policy process will not provide an adequate check on public power. Ideological and religious groups in government, for example, may use their discretionary power to force those of us who disagree with them to accept their vision of a "good society" and, in doing so, impose heavy costs on us.

The pursuit of narrow particularistic visions of the public interest, from the point of view of those exploited, is in this respect perhaps no less clearly selfish than the pursuit of material gain at their expense. Indeed, ideological, moral, or religious zealotry may be more likely to bring forth the exploitative character of government than the pursuit of narrow economic self-interest. Hayek's (1976) warning of "the immoral consequences of morally inspired efforts" remains relevant here (135). Herman Finer (1941) similarly suggests that we "must beware of the too good man as well as the too bad: each in his own way may give the public what it doesn't want" (338). The danger of such exploitation becomes especially great when society is deeply divided along ideological lines, as Aaron Wildavsky (1988) suggested is the case in the United States today.

It is worth noting, in this regard, that the Founders wrote not only of the "interests" but also of the "passions" of human beings. The constitution was seen as a means not simply of checking interests but also of checking passions. According to Madison, "neither moral nor religious motives can be relied on as an adequate control" (Wills 1982, 46). He argued that:

> A zeal for different opinions concerning religion, concerning Government and many other points, as well of speculations as of practice; an attachment to different leaders ambitiously contending for pre-eminence and power; or to persons of other descriptions whose fortunes have been interesting to the human passions, have in turn divided mankind into parties, inflamed them with mutual animosity, and rendered them much more disposed to vex and oppress each other, than to co-operate for their common good. So strong is this propensity

of mankind to fall into mutual animosities, that where no substantial occasion presents itself, the most frivolous and fanciful distinctions have been sufficient to kindle their unfriendly passions, and excite their most violent conflicts (44).

Also, Alexander Hamilton's argument for a nation dedicated to the pursuit of commerce was based on his view that the pursuit of commerce would dampen the destructive passions of citizens. He noted that "the spirit of commerce has a tendency to soften the manners of men and to extinguish those inflammable humours which have so often kindled into wars" (Wills 1982, 23).

Since we have conflicting values and interests, we may see that constitutional checks on power are necessary, therefore, not only to protect us against exploitation by those who would pursue their own material gain, but also to protect us against exploitation by those who would seek to pursue their own narrow vision of what is in our good. Constitutional checks on power then can be seen as a recognition in general of the simple fact, not that we are always selfish, but rather that we are fallible men and women and that any attempt to develop political institutions must come to grips with that fallibility.

UNINTENDED EXPLOITATION

The discussion so far has assumed that exploitation of citizens by government officials, whatever their motive, is intentional. In fact, given the limits of reason, we should expect there to be instances where government officials do not seek to exploit us but do so unintentionally. In this regard, it is worth emphasizing that the effects of many public policies are highly uncertain, particularly where policies change or modify private behavior, as is the case, for example, with economic policies, welfare policies, or educational policies. This uncertainty about the effects of public policy means that we may sometimes bear costs that were not originally anticipated by government officials. In other words, government officials may make errors. Hayek (1973) saw this when he warned that, because of the limits of our knowledge, "the more indirect and remote effects [of interventions] will mostly be unknown" (57) and that "many well-intentioned measures may have a long train of unforeseeable and undesirable consequences" (59). Burke (1955) likewise observed that "very plausible schemes, with very pleasing commencements, have often shameful and lamentable conclusions" (69).

Because of this uncertainty regarding the effects of public policies, constitutional rules, which limit the flexibility of government action, may then be seen as a desirable means of checking the discretionary power of government officials so as to limit the unforeseen costs of government policies. Hayek argued that rules in general are a mechanism by which societies cope with uncertainty. They are "adaptations to the impossibility of anyone taking conscious account of all the particular facts which enter into the order of society" (Hayek 1973, 13). This argument has been developed more formally by Ronald Heiner (1983), who suggests that when the consequences of human actions are highly uncertain so that costly errors are likely even with informed decision making, then it is rational for individuals to restrict their flexibility deliberately by relying on rules to guide their actions. In other words, when we are very unsure as to the consequences of our actions, then the costs of flexibility of action may exceed the benefits and it may make more sense simply to rely on existing rules. Heiner's argument is clearly relevant to the role of constitutional rules in limiting government discretion and, indeed, Heiner (1983) himself suggests that constitutionalism can be seen as "the design of rule-mechanisms to restrict the flexibility of government to react to whatever influences might prompt it to engage in vulnerable activities" (586).

We may desire constitutional rules then simply because we wish to limit the degree to which government officials may inadvertently exploit us as a result of errors. However, even if the effects of public policies were fully known, government officials might still unintentionally impose costs on us in exercising their discretionary power. This is because the discretionary actions of government officials are, by their very nature, unpredictable and create uncertainty. In general, the more flexibility that government officials have in deciding their actions, the more unpredictable are those actions. As Hayek (1944) noted, where the state has freedom to direct "the individual's actions so as to achieve particular ends," its actions must be decided "on the basis of the full circumstances of the moment" and will "therefore be unpredictable" (76).

This unpredictability of government actions is itself a cost for citizens, since it makes it more difficult for them to plan their own affairs. Madison saw this when he observed that it "poisons the blessings of liberty itself" if the laws "undergo such incessant changes that no man who knows what the law is to-day can guess what it will be to-morrow" (Wills 1982, 317). He argued that "an unstable government . . . damps every useful undertaking; the success and profit of which may depend on the continuance of existing arrangements" (317). It follows then that we may desire constitutional rules to check the discretionary power of government officials simply because, in order to plan our own actions, we desire a measure of predictability in the actions of government officials.

MAJORITY RULE

Among the most important constitutional rules that check the discretionary power of government officials are, of course, those providing for an electoral process based on majority rule. However, while important, there is good reason to believe that the electoral process alone cannot provide an adequate check on the discretionary power of government officials. Writers of an anti-rationalist bent have always been keenly aware of the dangers of unrestrained majority rule. Madison, for example, argued that "a dependence on the people is no doubt the primary controul on the government; but experience has taught mankind the necessity of auxiliary precautions" (Wills 1982, 262). Alexis de Tocqueville (1969) observed that "if you admit that a man vested with omnipotence can abuse it against his adversaries, why not admit the same concerning a majority?" (251). Lord Acton (1986) similarly warned that "the one pervading evil of democracy is the tyranny of the majority" (83). John Stuart Mill (1972), despite his rationalist inclinations, also warned of the dangers of majority rule. Mill observed that, given majority rule, the people "may desire to oppress a part of their number; and precautions are as much needed against this, as against any other abuse of power" (72).

In terms of the logic of a constitution, unrestrained majority rule does not prevent the exploitation of citizens by government but rather gives it a new form. In particular, unrestrained majority rule means that individuals and groups in society will be motivated, either by their interests or by their passions, to form coalitions to secure policies that benefit or please them without regard to the costs of those policies to others. To put it in economic terms again, the majority may impose negative externalities on the minority (Buchanan and Tullock 1962). For example, where legislative majorities are free to use their discretion to determine how the tax burden is to be shared among individuals, they can use the budget to obtain those goods and services that they desire from government and, at the same time, shift the cost of financing such goods and services to others.

Under these conditions, majority rule is no longer a device for expressing any coherent general will of the community or even the will of the majority. Rather majority rule simply becomes a device by which various groups in society can advance their objectives at the expense of other citizens. Elected leaders in this process become simply brokers of interests and causes as they seek to use their discretion to please those groups whose support they need for reelection. Majority rule then can become the pretext for little more than elective despotism.

Hayek (1979b) saw the defects of unrestrained majority rule clearly when he argued that unrestrained majority rule results in "handing over unlimited power to a group of elected representatives whose decisions must be guided by the exigencies of a bargaining process in which elected representatives bribe a sufficient number of voters to support an organized group of themselves numerous enough to outvote the rest" (4–5). Hayek argued that "corrupt at the same time weak, . . . the governing majority must do what it can do to gratify the wishes of the groups from which it needs support, however harmful to the rest such measures may be" and that "it is wholly incapable of pursuing a consistent course of action, lurching like a steamroller driven by one who is drunk" (11). Majority rule simply becomes a means of "distributing the booty which can be extracted from a dissident minority" (139).

This criticism of unrestrained majority rule should not be misinterpreted as opposition or hostility to democratic processes. Majority rule provides an essential and desirable check on the arbitrary exercise of government power. As Hayek (1979b) argued, majority rule "serves as a protection against despotism and tyranny . . . a convention which mainly serves to prevent harm" (133). Also, Burke (1993) observed that, without popular elections, "the people cannot long enjoy the substance of freedom" (145). Majority rule, as a check on power, means that the actions of government should be acceptable to the majority of citizens. However, this is not the same thing as arguing that the majority is entitled to enact any measure that it pleases. Herbert Spencer (1982), the nineteenth century social theorist, suggested that the idea of unlimited parliamentary authority was really a reincarnation of the old "divine right of kings" as "the divine right of parliaments" and was no more than a "Great Political Superstition" (123). Certainly, given that even a majority must consist of fallible men and women, there would seem a necessity for constitutional rules, beyond those providing for elections, so as to check the discretionary power of even democratically elected government officials.

John Locke (1939b), despite his assertion that the legislature "be the supreme power in every commonwealth" (457), saw the logic of restraining majority power when he argued that legislative power could not "possibly be absolutely arbitrary over the lives and fortunes of the people" and that "nobody has an absolute arbitrary power over himself, or over any other to destroy his own life, or take away the life and property of another" (457). Rather, according to Locke, the legislature "is bound to dispense justice, and decide the rights of the subject by promulgated standing laws, and known authorized judges" (458). Locke further believed in a separation of executive and legislative power. He observed that "it may be too great a temptation to human frailty, apt to grasp at power for the same persons, who have the power of making laws, to have also in their hands the power to execute them" (462).

The idea that the discretionary power of elected officials should be checked may be seen by some as violating popular sovereignty or as frustrating the expression of Rousseau's general will. In other words, checks on the discretionary power of elected officials may be viewed as restricting the ability of a sovereign people to speak and act freely for themselves through their elected representatives. This was, as we have seen, the view of many early public administration writers, who opposed the separation of powers, and is widely held today. However, as noted above, unrestrained majority rule does not necessarily represent any general will even of a majority of the people. Rather, it often reflects simply the separate and particular interests of those groups who happen to comprise the majority on a particular issue. Furthermore, a preoccupation with the question of sovereignty would seem entirely misdirected in a constitutional system in which, as we have noted, Madison argued that "the constant aim is to divide and arrange the several offices in such a manner as that each may be a check on the other" (Wills 1982, 263). As Popper (1966a) has pointed out, the appropriate question here should be not "Who should rule?" but rather "How can we so organize political institutions that bad and incompetent rulers can be prevented from doing too much damage?" (121).

THE USE OF KNOWLEDGE

The foregoing arguments for constitutional checks on the discretionary power of government officials are essentially negative. Checks on discretionary power are seen as means of limiting the potentially exploitative power of government, whether exercised deliberately or unintentionally. The negative character of these arguments is consistent with an anti-rationalist perspective and, in my view, these arguments taken alone present a compelling logical case for checking power constitutionally. However, I believe that the argument for checking power can be framed in a somewhat more positive fashion. In particular, a case can be made that the existence of constitutional checks on power within a political system permits and even encourages the use of a greater amount and broader array of knowledge about policies and their possible effects than would occur in the absence of such checks; knowledge that may sometimes lead to better policies overall.

The work of Hayek is again instructive here. According to Hayek (1948), whatever are the requirements for an effective social order, knowledge of these is never available to a single mind. No single individual or central authority can know what information is required to rationally plan and direct the use of resources in society or where that information might be obtained. The basic problem for society, according to Hayek (1948), is "the utilization of knowledge which is not given to anyone in its totality" (78). The problem here is not simply the sheer volume of knowledge but also its character. Much of the knowledge necessary to run an effective social order is practical in nature and based in experience rather than scientific analysis. It consists of what individuals have thought it to their advantage to discover and use in particular situations. This knowledge is also subjective in nature in that it consists not of a single agreed upon set of "facts" as such, but rather of differing views of the "facts." Such knowledge, as Hayek (1979a) noted, can never exist "as an integrated whole" ready for use by some central authority, but consists rather of the "separate and often inconsistent and even conflicting views of different people" (92).

This type of knowledge, according to Hayek, can only be obtained through decentralized systems of human interaction. Decentralization provides the opportunities and incentives for individuals to acquire and use practical knowledge relevant to their particular needs. Decentralization also provides greater opportunities and incentives for individuals to adjust their different views of the facts to each other and to reality. Such opportunities and incentives would not exist were decisions to be made by a single individual or group of individuals. As a result, much relevant information would never be known let alone used in a centralized system of economic and social decision making.

The necessity for decentralization as a means of acquiring and using knowledge forms the basis of Hayek's arguments for a market order or catallaxy as he termed it. However, its relevance would seem to extend beyond the market. In particular, a constitutional system of government, by decentralizing political power, can help promote the use of knowledge in the political process.

Constitutional checks on power, as noted earlier, provide a system of multiple veto points in the political process. These veto points limit the ability of any particular group of political leaders to simply impose its will on others in the political process. As a result, constitutional checks on power force political leaders to take account of information and opinions held by others about the effects of public policies. This may occur as a result of a process of dialogue in which individuals acquire and exchange knowledge about policies as they seek to persuade each other of the merits of their positions. However, even where this ideal is not realized, knowledge about the effects of particular policies is still used by individuals in determining which particular policies best advance their interests. As a result, this knowledge about the effects of policies affects their positions and actions on particular policies and so affects policy outcomes.

What is suggested here is something akin to the process of mutual adjustment in politics, as described by Michael Polanyi (Polanyi and Prosch 1975) and Charles Lindblom (1959, 1990). In such a process, political actors are forced to accommodate their positions on policy to the positions of others and, in doing so, are led to take account of knowledge held by others regarding the effects of policies. Such a system of mutual adjustment is obviously imperfect in that much relevant knowledge about the effects of particular policies may not be used in the political process, either because it does not meet the needs or interests of those participating in the process, or because it is possessed by individuals who lack access to the political process. However, in assessing the value of a constitutional system in promoting the use of knowledge, we should not compare it with some hypothetical rationalist ideal of an omniscient benevolent despot.

In this regard, it may be reasonably argued that a constitutional system of checking power results in the use of a greater volume and array of knowledge than either could or would be used by a single political leader or single group of leaders, relying on their own limited knowledge and driven by their own interests and passions. As Lindblom (1959) has argued, a system of mutual adjustment "often can assure a more comprehensive regard for the values of the whole society than any attempt at intellectual comprehensiveness" (85). The Scottish philosopher Adam Ferguson (1980) made a similar point over two centuries ago when he argued that "the wisest laws are never, perhaps, dictated by the interest and spirit of any order of men; they are moved, they are opposed, or amended, by different hands; and come at last to express that medium and composition which contending parties have forced one another to adopt" (128).

We have argued then that constitutional checks on the discretionary power of government officials are desirable not only because they serve to limit the costs that government imposes upon us but also because they can promote the use of more knowledge about the effects of public policies. It is interesting to note here, therefore, that this logic of a constitution seems to apply both in the case of relatively cynical views of the political process and in the case of relatively idealistic views of the political process. Whether we assume that political actors pursue their self-interest or their vision of the public interest, it is reasonable that we should seek constitutional checks on political power. Whether we view the political process as one of reconciling existing interests and passions or one of promoting fuller use of knowledge, it is also reasonable that we should seek checks on political power. The logical argument for constitutional rules that check power, therefore, would seem quite robust and merits perhaps more serious consideration and appreciation than it has typically been given by writers in public administration.

CONCLUSION

We have explored in this chapter the question as to why we, as a community of reasonable but fallible individuals, should seek constitutional limits to check the discretionary power of government officials. This analysis suggests that constitutional checks on power are desirable, even where power is exercised by democratically elected leaders, because of the fallibility of human beings and as a means of promoting the use of knowledge in the political process. This exploration of the arguments for checking power suggests that not only are constitutional checks on power consistent with our political tradition, but they can also be defended on a variety of logical grounds. It is in light of this logic that the constitutional mechanisms devised by the Founders can be seen and appreciated. The separation of powers, federalism, a bicameral legislature, and the Bill of Rights all, for example, provide particular mechanisms to check the discretionary power of government officials. An appreciation of the logic of a constitution does not substitute for, but rather reinforces an appreciation of the political tradition of the Founders.

This is not to argue that any examination of the logic of a constitution leads to a prescription for a unique optimal structure of government. We may each see various possible combinations of constitutional mechanisms as desirable means of checking power. Hayek (1979b), for example, proposed a model constitution in the British context that was quite different from the U.S. Constitution. Much will depend here on the particular political tradition of a country. An understanding of the logic of a constitution simply reminds us that in constitutional discussions about the structure and process of government, we should, as the Founders' arguments did, pay significant attention to the problem of checking power.

5
Visions of Public Administration

In the last chapter, the logic of the anti-rationalist argument for constitutional checks on power was examined. If we accept this logic, the question arises then as to what kind of public administration would be consistent with a constitutional system directed at checking power. It is important to emphasize here that public administration, as the provider of public services to citizens, plays a key role in determining the type of government with which citizens must deal. How government affects the lives of citizens depends on the actions of public administrators.

Alexander Hamilton saw this when he observed that "the true test of a good government is its aptitude and tendency to produce a good administration" (Wills 1982, 347), as did the Anti-Federalist John DeWitt, when he argued that "the only excellency of any government is in exact proportion to the administration of it" (Ketcham 1986, 193). Hegel (1952) similarly observed that "it is on the conduct of officials that there depend . . . the execution—or alternatively the distortion and frustration—of state projects" (192). In other words, public administration can be an institution by which government serves or burdens citizens. Government can serve citizens only through the actions of public administrators. Similarly, government can exploit citizens only through the actions of public administrators. The character of administrative actions determines in significant part the character of government.

If we accept that a constitutional system directed at checking political power is a valued aspect of government, it is important that the structure and process of public administration reflect that value. It may be useful to begin here by examining existing visions of public administration, which have been proposed by public administration writers, and see to what extent these take adequate account of the need to check power. By doing this, we can gain insight into the strengths and deficiencies of existing visions and, thereby, gain also a better appreciation of the necessary elements of an anti-rationalist vision of public administration.

"DISCRETIONISTS" AND "INSTRUMENTALISTS"

The literature in public administration is obviously diverse and no simple classification can do justice to it entirely. However, it seems fair to suggest

54

that this literature has tended to focus around two different visions of public administration. The first, termed here a "discretionist" vision, sees public administration as almost an independent or autonomous agent for the advancement of government actions that promote the "public interest." According to this vision, public administrators should use their own properly informed and ethically guided notions of what is in the public interest to guide their actions. The second, which might be termed an "instrumentalist" vision, sees public administration almost entirely as an instrument of the political will of a community, as expressed through its elected political leaders. Public administrators, according to this vision, must ascertain and carry out the wishes of the elected representatives of the people.

The issues that separate discretionists and instrumentalists were probably most clearly articulated in a lively written debate between Carl Friedrich (1940) and Herman Finer (1941). This debate, although now over half a century old, raises points still remarkably germane to contemporary disagreements about the role of public administration. It will be helpful, therefore, to review their work here and to examine it in light of the anti-rationalist emphasis on checking power.

THE FRIEDRICH ARGUMENT

Friedrich, who may best be described as a discretionist, argued that the external checks exercised by elected political leaders could no longer be relied upon to provide adequate control over the actions of public administrators. According to Friedrich (1940), "parliamentary responsibility is largely inoperative and certainly ineffectual" (10). He argued that substantial administrative discretion is unavoidable, noting that "even under the best arrangements a considerable margin of irresponsible conduct of administrative activities is inevitable" (3). Friedrich here, it should be made clear, was not criticizing the conduct of administrators, but simply noting the inevitable fact that public administrators are not always answerable to anybody in particular for their actions. Indeed, far from criticizing administrators, Friedrich saw them as more able to deal effectively with the public policy problems of a nation than popularly elected legislators. In Friedrich's view, the nature of the problems facing modern governments is "so novel and complex" that they call for "creative solutions" for which the popular will can provide little guidance. According to Friedrich:

> The pious formulas about the will of the people are all very well, but when it comes to these issues of social maladjustment the popular will

has little content, except the desire to see such maladjustments removed. A solution which fails in this regard, or which causes new and perhaps greater maladjustments is bad; we have a right to call such a policy irresponsible if it can be shown that it was adopted without proper regard to the existing sum of human knowledge concerning the technical issues involved; we also have a right to call it irresponsible if it can be shown that it was adopted without proper regard for existing preferences in the community, and more particularly its prevailing majority (12).

Friedrich argued here that public administrators, in exercising their inevitable discretion must have a "dual standard of administrative responsibility." They must be responsive to both technical knowledge and popular sentiment. The internal commitment of public administrators to these technical and political standards is what, for Friedrich, ensures administrative responsibility. They provide "inner checks" on the behavior of public administrators so that responsibility here "is not so much enforced as it is elicited" (19).

The responsiveness of public administrators to standards of technical knowledge, in Friedrich's view, cannot be accomplished by responsibility to elected officials but can only occur when their hypotheses are "subjected to thorough scrutiny by their colleagues in what is known as the 'fellowship of science'" (12). In other words, public administrators should have a responsibility to the scientific community. According to Friedrich:

the fact remains that throughout the length and breadth of our technical civilization there is arising a type of responsibility on the part of the permanent administrator, the man who is called upon to seek and find creative solutions for our crying technical needs, which cannot be effectively enforced except by fellow-technicians who are capable of judging his policy in terms of the scientific knowledge bearing upon it. "Nature's laws are always enforced," and a public policy which neglects them is bound to come to grief, no matter how eloquently it may be advocated by popular orators, eager partisans, or smart careerists (14).

The actions of public administrators to be responsible must then satisfy the canons of science. At the same time, Friedrich believed that "technical responsibility is not sufficient to keep a civil service wholesome and zealous, and that political responsibility is needed to produce truly responsible policy in a popular government" (14). The standards of responsibility must be both technical and political. However, Friedrich did not believe that legislative control, on its own, is adequate to ensure political responsibility because of the "intrusion of party politics" and "the tremendous difficulty which the public encounters in trying to grasp the broader implications of policy issues" (14).

Friedrich looked rather to alternative political devices for ensuring administrative responsibility. He noted, with approval, that "newer and equally potent instruments have been developed in recent years" (16). These included, for Friedrich, the educational and promotional activities of public agencies, direct citizen contacts with agencies, and referenda or polling of citizens affected by particular policies, such as were conducted by the United States Department of Agriculture. Friedrich was in favor of what he termed "direct citizen participation in policy formulation at the administrative level" to compensate "for the gradual disappearance of effective legislation by individual members of legislative assemblies" (18). Instead of "subserviency to arbitrary will," Friedrich argued, what we require is "responsiveness to commonly felt needs and wants" (20).

Friedrich further believed that technical standards of responsibility authorized and, indeed, required public administrators to speak out publicly on policy issues—"to submit their views to outside criticism" (22). Neither did he believe that public administrators should confine themselves to discussions of facts since, for Friedrich, "facts and policies cannot be separated" (22). He saw no value in "gag rules" on the utterances of public administrators. According to Friedrich:

> In matters of vital importance the general public is entitled to the views of its permanent servants. Such views may often provide a salutary check on partisan extravagances. Such views should be available not only to the executive but to the legislature and the public as well (23).

The only standard that Friedrich was prepared to apply to the public statements of public administrators was to insist that they "be in keeping with the highest requirements of scientific work" (23). Appearing to draw again on this idea of a "fellowship of science," he argued that "if a man's superiors disagree with him, let them mount the same rostrum and prove that he is wrong; before the goddess of science all men are equal" (23).

Friedrich's view of public administration is in many ways prototypical of the discretionist point of view. There is a critique of the effectiveness of conventional political mechanisms. Administrative discretion is seen as a remedy for ineffective government. There is an appeal not only to the technical competence but also to the political competence of administrators. Finally, there is a faith in the ability and inclination of public administrators to discern and act on what is in the public interest. Little if any concern is expressed about the potential for abuse of discretion by public administrators. This view, while by no means dominant in the field, can be found across a fairly broad spectrum of contemporary literature on public administration. Contemporary discretionists often exhibit perhaps less faith in conventional science than did Friedrich, but they nonetheless claim a special competence for public administration and call for a more active role for public administrators in what they believe is a seriously flawed political process.

George Frederickson (1971), for example, in arguing for the "new Public Administration" asserts that "the procedures of representative democracy presently operate in a way that either fails or only very gradually attempts to reverse systematic discrimination against disadvantaged minorities" and that, therefore, administrators must "work for changes which try to redress the deprivation of minorities" and pursue activities "designed to enhance the political power and economic well-being of these minorities" (311). Perhaps the clearest statements of this discretionist position can be found in a recent volume of readings edited by Henry Kass and Bayard Catron (1990), which argues that the "sense of political community" in the United States "has been severely eroded by the extreme pluralism that characterizes contemporary American politics" (12). These authors, all coming from quite different philosophical perspectives, call for administrators to "escape the narrow technical-instrumental role in which they have often been cast," and to "help restore a shared sense of political community" by taking "a leading role in resolving those ethical issues of justice and welfare that are always present in the process of constructing a community" (12–13).

Charles Fox and Clarke Cochrane, whose paper is included in the Kass and Catron volume, take perhaps the strongest position when they argue that public administration should be what they see as a moderate version of Plato's guardian class. According to Fox and Cochrane (1990):

> Electoral politics engages either those particularistic interests or policy-irrelevant social, cultural and religious norms, none of which can claim more than a small point on the spectrum of the public interest. City councils are generally not much more than the decaying residues of once vibrant old-boy networks of localized petit bourgeois. Into this vacuum march professionally trained, sophisticated, socially aware, and virtuous public administrators . . . Better them, we say, than the existing alternative (107).

THE FINER ARGUMENT

Herman Finer (1941) clearly articulated the instrumentalist view, of which Friedrich was so critical, when he argued that "the servants of the public are not to decide their own course; they are to be responsible to the elected representatives of the public, and these are to determine the course of action of the public servants to the most minute degree that is technically feasible" (336). In Finer's view, "we must require principally and austerely the subservience of the public official" to elected officials (342). Finer did not believe that a public administrator's sense of responsibility to either technical knowledge or political sentiment could provide any adequate check on administrative actions. He argued that:

> Moral responsibility is likely to operate in direct proportion to the strictness and efficiency of political responsibility, and to fall away into all sorts of perversions when the latter is weakly enforced. While professional standards, duty to the public, and pursuit of technological efficiency are factors in sound administrative operation, they are but ingredients, and not continuously motivating factors, of sound policy, and they require public and political control and direction (350).

According to Finer, the securing of political and administrative responsibility in a democracy requires three conditions:

> First, the mastership of the public, in the sense that politicians and employees are working not for the good of the public in the sense of what the public needs, but of the wants of the public as expressed by the public. Second, recognition that this mastership needs institutions, and particularly the centrality of an elected organ, for its expression and the exertion of its authority. More important than these two is the third notion, namely that the function of the public and of its elected institutions is not merely the exhibition of its mastership by informing governments and officials of what it wants, but the authority and power to exercise an effect upon the course which the latter are to pursue, the power to exact obedience to orders (337).

In Finer's view, responsibility then is meaningless unless elected leaders have the power to ensure that public administrators follow their wishes and directives. According to Finer, "sooner or later there is an abuse of power when external punitive controls are lacking" (337). This abuse of power by government officials may take the form of "nonfeasance" where "they have not done what law or custom required them to do," "malfeasance, where a duty is carried out with waste and damage," or "overfeasance, where a duty is undertaken beyond what law and custom oblige or empower" (337–338). Finer, as noted in the last chapter, seemed to exhibit particular concern with overfeasance. He argued that "a system which gives the 'good' man freedom of action, in the expectation of benefiting from all the 'good' he has in him, must sooner or later (since no man is without faults) cause his faults to be loaded on to the public also" (338).

Finer acknowledged Friedrich's point that the controls exercised over public administrators by elected officials might, in fact, be inadequate but he saw this as indicating the need to develop more effective legislative controls. According to Finer, the "various drawbacks of political control can be remedied" (340). He argued that these drawbacks did not mean, as Friedrich seemed to suggest, "that the administration should be given its head, but on the contrary that legislative bodies should be improved" (340). Finer suggested that "conceding the growing power of officials we may discover the remedy in the improvement of the quality of political parties and elections, if our minds are ready to explore" (340).

Finer also conceded that "an external agency could not attend to every administrative particular" and that "some latitude" for discretion "must be given" (340). He saw no harm in "devices" for eliciting public opinion but insisted that these must be auxiliary means of political control. "All these devices have their value" but, according to Finer, "they do not and cannot commit and compel the official to change his course" (341). Finer was afraid that the adoption of Friedrich's vision of technical and political responsibility for public administrators would result in "the enhancement of official conceit and what has come to be known as the 'new despotism'" (340).

Neither did Finer accept Friedrich's view that legislative control was "largely inoperative and certainly ineffectual." He provided examples of what he termed "the outstanding successes" of Parliament in controlling government (345). Finer thought "the public and the political assemblies . . . adequately sagacious to direct policy" (350). He accused Friedrich of adopting "quite an undemocratic view of government" and of throwing "scorn upon the popular will" (346). Finer suggested that "the will of the people has content, not only about what it desires, but how maladjustments can be remedied" (346). He argued that the "sagacity" of legislative assemblies "is not to be ignored or derided" (346).

Finer was also less than enthusiastic about Friedrich's notion that public administrators could be held accountable for their actions to the "fellowship of science" (347). He wondered what would happen if public administrators happened to disagree with the opinions of their learned colleagues or how public administrators were to deal with conflicting professional and scientific advice. Finer thought that Friedrich, in general, attached far too much importance to contemporary technical knowledge. He suggested that technical solutions for public problems had "for centuries been offered by the experts of various kinds" and that "the verdict of mankind has been that they need the expert on tap and not on top" (348).

Finally, Finer was critical of Friedrich's idea that public administrators should make their policy differences with elected leaders publicly known. He thought it perfectly possible to distinguish facts from policy, and that the public administrator should "confine himself to frank private demonstration of the alternatives and their advantages and disadvantages, to his political chief, or where the political system requires, to the committee of the assembly at their request" (349). Public disclosure of policy differences would, according to Finer, set up the public administrator against elected officials and "he would certainly be kicked out by the legislature or chief executive, and it would serve him right" (349). He believed that "democracy is ill served by and justifiably abhors those who, appointed to be its servants, assume the status and demeanor of masters" (349).

In his critique of Friedrich, Finer captures three key elements of the instrumentalist point of view. Firstly, in the absence of external checks, public administrators cannot be trusted to act in the public interest and may be expected to abuse their authority. Secondly, the will of the people has real content and that content is expressed first and foremost through its elected representatives. Thirdly, democracy requires, therefore, that public administrators carry out the wishes of the people's elected representatives and be subject to punishment if they do not. No questions are raised here regarding the content of the public will or the problems associated with the abuse of power by elected authorities.

This idea that public administrators should carry out the will of elected leaders was fundamental to early public administration thought in the United States. It is clearly implied in the politics-administration dichotomy asserted by early public administration writers, including Woodrow Wilson (1955) and Frank Goodnow (1900). According to Wilson (1955), "administration lies outside the proper sphere of politics" (14). Its role for Wilson is the "detailed and systematic execution of public law" (15). While early writers were undoubtedly as concerned with keeping corrupt politicians out of administration as with keeping administrators out of politics, they seemed to accept the implication of the dichotomy that elected leaders and not public administrators should determine policy. In Wilson's (1955) view, "we could grant democracy the sufficient honor of ultimately determining by debate all essential questions affecting the public weal, of basing all structures of policy upon the major will" (20).

The politics-administration dichotomy has long since been discredited by public administration writers such as Paul Appleby (1945). However, the idea that public administrators should follow the wishes and directives of elected officials is still pervasive. Indeed, this notion of strict democratic accountability would seem to remain an article of faith, strongly held while not always clearly stated, for many if not most writers in public administration. It is implicit in the instrumental rationalism of Herbert Simon (1945) and other writers in the mainstream who focus on the role of public administration in the efficient execution of public objectives, leaving to the political process the task of formulating such objectives. More explicitly, it forms the basis for Theodore Lowi's (1979) vision of juridical democracy in which Congress would be forced to clearly state the purposes and means of public programs and to minimize administrative discretion. A notion of strict democratic accountability also underlies Richard Nathan's (1976) advocacy of an "Administrative Presidency" to exercise more effective managerial control over the actions of public administrators and Ronald Moe's (1990) suggestion that the executive branch should return to traditional hierarchical principles of organization to promote greater legal and political accountability.

John Burke (1986) provides perhaps one of the most forceful contemporary arguments for strict democratic accountability. While noting some limited exceptions to the strict democratic accountability of public administrators, he clearly rejects the idea that public administrators should play any significant independent role in the process of policy formulation and argues in general for the obedience of administrators to the wishes of elected leaders. According to Burke (1986), "The decisions made by relevant political authorities, institutions and processes" must "determine the general obligations and duties of subordinate officials" (39). This vision, therefore, of public administration as largely an instrument of the will of elected leaders remains strong.

THE FRIEDRICH-FINER DEBATE AND THE CHECKING OF POWER

From an anti-rationalist perspective, the visions of public administration advanced by Friedrich and Finer have both their merits and defects. Friedrich's characterization of "the pious formulas about the will of the people" may sound undemocratic to modern ears, but is not inconsistent with the anti-rationalist argument that citizens have conflicting interests and passions and are often unlikely to agree as to what constitutes the public good. Also, his advocacy of "direct citizen participation in policy formation at the administrative level" would seem to provide an opportunity for citizens, who see themselves as harmed or potentially harmed by government policies, to at least make their views known to administrators. As such, this type of citizen participation is consistent with the arguments for checking power advanced in chapter four. Finally, Friedrich seemed to appreciate the need to check the power of elected majorities when he suggested that the public airing of differences between administrators and elected officials might serve as "a salutory check on partisan extravagances."

On the other hand, Friedrich's notion that responsibility "is not so much enforced as it is elicited" would seem to give insufficient weight to the potential problem of abuse of authority and the exploitation of citizens by public administrators exercising relatively unfettered discretion. Certainly, the "inner checks" upon which he based his notion of administrative responsibility are important, as I shall argue later, but whether they are sufficient to check the abuse of power by administrators is open to serious question. Responsibility to "fellow-technicians" and "direct citizen participation in policy formation at the administrative level" may provide guidance but cannot alone adequately check administrative power. If we accept that public administrators, like all of us, are fallible, then a moral commitment to the "dual standard" of technical knowledge and popular sentiment alone cannot prevent the abuse of power and external checks on power would seem necessary. Without such checks, Finer's concern over the "enhancement of official conceit" and the "new despotism" would seem well founded.

Furthermore, Friedrich placed excessive emphasis on the value of the scientific knowledge possessed by public administrators and gave perhaps insufficient emphasis to the value of the practical knowledge and opinions of elected representatives and citizens regarding the effects of public policies. As indicated in chapter four, no single individual has the wisdom to run a social order. Charles Lindblom (1959) argues that an administrator cannot "be competent on all policies" and "cannot even comprehend one policy entirely" (84). Debate within the "fellowship of science" can certainly be helpful, but cannot take account of all of the knowledge relevant to consideration of public policies.

As noted in chapter one, the social sciences upon which many public administrators rely for their expertise provide few clear and indisputable guidelines for public policy. Also, scientists and professionals are fallible human beings so that their opinions are inevitably affected by both their own interests and their own narrow particularistic visions of the public good. The knowledge possessed by scientific experts then is inevitably both uncertain and biased to some degree. Furthermore, given such uncertainty and bias, this expertise, when backed by political power, can too easily become a pretext for exploitative actions on the part of public administrators. In this regard, Finer was correct in asserting that the expert should be kept "on tap and not on top."

However, while Finer's critiques of Friedrich's argument for relatively unfettered administrative discretion were often quite consistent with the anti-rationalist emphasis on the need to check power, his own vision was not. His argument that "the will of the people has content" may be true on occasion but it overlooks what anti-rationalists would see as an often inevitable diversity of individual interests, passions, and opinions. Furthermore, by requiring "principally and austerely the subservience of the public official" to elected officials and by proposing that the actions of public administrators be controlled "to the most minute degree that is technically feasible," Finer was clearly advocating not simply that the actions of government should be acceptable to the majority but that the majority should always get precisely what it wants. This is, as argued in chapter four, a troublesome proposition from an anti-rationalist perspective and, furthermore, is explicitly inconsistent with the writings of the Founders.

Finer did not show any appreciation that the content of the "will of the people" as expressed through the political process may consist sometimes merely of a desire of the majority to exploit a minority for economic, religious, or ideological purposes. It did not bother him that the subservient administrators who give exact obedience to their elected leaders might simply become the efficient tool of an exploitative majority. Indeed, Finer seemed quite willing to consider ways of further strengthening legislative control over administration should it be found lacking; ways, which from an anti-rationalist perspective, would render it a more effective and efficient weapon for an exploitative majority. Finer, in short, appeared oblivious to the problems associated with unrestrained majority rule. He was rightly sensitive to the problem of abuse of power by public administrators, but did not seem to see that precisely the same problem of abuse of power could exist in the case of power wielded by elected leaders.

To be fair to Finer, his critique of unfettered administrative discretion reveals, in this regard, a keen, characteristically English, and essentially anti-rationalist sense of the limits of reason and human nature. However, enamored by dangerously simplistic nineteenth century notions of parliamentary sovereignty, he failed to follow through on the logical implications of such limits for the exercise of power by very human legislators. Finer did not seem to worry that legislators might not always exhibit "sagacity" but rather might sometimes be capable of precisely the same type of "official conceit" in their actions as public administrators. In other words, his own assertion that "no man is without faults" was apparently of little concern to him when it came to the wishes of democratically elected majorities and their leaders. As a result, in his zeal to warn us of the dangers of a bureaucratic "new despotism," Finer seemed to end up endorsing an elective despotism.

The visions of public administration then, advanced by Friedrich and Finer, each raise serious problems from an anti-rationalist perspective. Both seem to appreciate the need to check power but are selective as to where those checks should be placed. In other words, Friedrich and Finer each have a blind spot with respect to the desirability of checking discretionary power. Friedrich seems relatively unconcerned about the need to check the discretionary power of public administrators and Finer seems relatively unconcerned about the need to check the power of democratically elected leaders. As a result, each presents a vision for public administration that is problematic. Friedrich's vision raises the specter of an exploitative bureaucratic Leviathan accountable to nobody except itself and out of control. Finer's vision, on the other hand, raises the possibility of public administrators simply being, what Alexander Hamilton termed, "obsequious instruments" of their master's "pleasure" (Wills 1982, 386). In this regard, it is ironic that Finer (1941) should use the example of Nazi Germany to help make his case for democratic responsibility (337), since it can reasonably be argued that the evils of Nazism were exacerbated if not caused by an overly obedient public administration (Frederickson and Hart 1985).

It should perhaps not surprise us that neither Friedrich's discretionist vision nor Finer's instrumentalist vision should prove satisfactory from an anti-rationalist perspective. Both visions, when carefully considered, seem at root rationalist in nature. Friedrich saw government as guided best by the technically and politically informed reason of sophisticated, trained, and morally upright public administrators. In this regard, Friedrich's views seem to echo those of John Stuart Mill (1972) who argued that a democracy must be "willing that the work which requires skill should be done by those who possess it" (267). Finer, on the other hand, saw government as guided best by the reason exercised not by administrators but by democratically elected legislators. Finer would seem to support Jean-Jacques Rousseau's view (1987) that the will of the executive body "is not and should not be anything other than the general will or the law" (176). The debate between Friedrich and Finer is, therefore, more about whose reason should prevail in a democracy than about how to govern in a society in which the powers of reason of both public administrators and legislators are severely limited.

CONCLUSION

If we accept the anti-rationalist argument that political power, whatever its source, should be checked, then neither the discretionist nor the instrumentalist visions of public administration would seem acceptable. It may be argued that in focusing here on the Friedrich-Finer debate, I have missed important new points raised by modern discretionists and instrumentalists. However, as has been shown, the key issues raised in this debate are still very much with us today. Modern discretionists generally give little weight to concerns about the abuse of power by administrators and modern instrumentalists generally give little weight to concerns about the abuse of power by elected leaders.

In the final analysis, Friedrich's and Finer's visions of the role of public administration are both useful in reminding us that public administrators can exploit citizens in two ways. Firstly, public administrators can be a source of exploitation of citizens through the independent exercise of their own discretion. Secondly, through the failure to exercise discretion, they can become the instruments of exploitation of citizens for political leaders. What is required, from an anti-rationalist perspective, is a vision then of public administration that steers an admittedly difficult course between the visions of Friedrich and Finer; a vision that acknowledges the possibility of abuses of power on the part of both elected officials and public administrators, and that recognizes the necessity of checking the power of each.

6

An Anti-rationalist Vision of Public Administration

If neither the discretionist vision of Carl Friedrich nor the instrumentalist vision of Herman Finer regarding the role of public administration would seem acceptable from an anti-rationalist perspective, then what should an anti-rationalist public administration look like? The key to answering this question, in my view, is to recognize firstly that public administrators must be free to exercise some significant amount of discretion with respect to public policy. Administrative discretion can be justified on the grounds that it sometimes permits public administrators to modify, delay, or resist the directives of political leaders in a lawful manner. Such actions are necessary on occasion if public administrators are to avoid becoming simply instruments of exploitation for various political leaders. The exercise of administrative discretion can also encourage a greater use of both the technical and practical knowledge possessed by public administrators regarding the effects of public policies. To the extent that public administrators are permitted through the exercise of administrative discretion to play an active role in the shaping of public policy, it is more likely that such policy will reflect their knowledge.

Secondly, we must recognize that, because public administrators are no less fallible than political leaders, we need also to check the discretionary power of administrators. Such checks are necessary so that administrative discretion, whether exercised out of self-interest or a concern for the public good, is not itself a source of exploitation. Checks on administrative discretion should also serve to encourage administrators to take account of a broader range of knowledge in taking administrative actions. What is required then is a type of public administration that is capable of checking power but is, at the same time, checked itself. This chapter seeks to provide at least the outlines of such a public administration.

ADMINISTRATIVE DISCRETION AND CHECKING POWER

To suggest that public administrators should check the discretionary power of political leaders may be seen somehow as undemocratic, given that public administrators are not elected officials. However, as we have seen in chapter four, checks on the power of even democratically elected political leaders are necessary from an anti-rationalist perspective. In light of this, there would seem no a priori reason why such checks on power should not include the exercise of significant administrative discretion. Indeed, given that public administration significantly determines whether government will serve or exploit its citizens, administrative discretion would seem a necessary element in any constitutional system directed at checking power. It is not advocated here that public administrators should ignore the legal directives of their political leaders. However, public administrators can check the power of political leaders by raising questions with political leaders, by trying to persuade them to sometimes change course, and by interpreting political directives in a fashion that permits them to limit the costs imposed upon citizens.

Administrative discretion within a constitutional order can be secured in at least two ways. Firstly, it is desirable that neither the executive nor the legislative branches of government should have absolute authority over the actions of public administrators. Absolute command over public administration by any one branch of government, while more conducive to the achievement of its particular goals, must increase significantly the risk that some citizens will be exploited by that branch through the actions of public administrators. Therefore, there is much to be said for having public administrators accountable to more than one political master. Mixed or shared accountability means that when there is a disagreement between different branches of government on some policy matter, then public administrators can exercise discretion in regard to which branch's policy is implemented. Such discretion makes it possible for public administrators to avoid being used as an instrument of exploitation by choosing among their political masters.

Mixed accountability does, of course, violate the maxim of unity of command; a maxim that was central to early public administration thinking (Gulick and Urwick 1937). However, unity of command makes sense only if one presupposes some sovereign general will that should be implemented. Such a presupposition is unacceptable from an anti-rationalist perspective because it fails to recognize the inevitable diversity of interests and passions, expressed through the political process, and the fundamental necessity of checking power. Therefore, unity of command, except in special circumstances such as military actions or emergency disaster relief, would also seem unacceptable from an anti-rationalist perspective.

In addition to mixed accountability, administrative discretion can also be secured through the creation of a career civil service. Clearly, one of the most important forms of control that political leaders can exert over the actions of public administrators is the power to substantially affect their economic livelihood. Discretion in following the directives of political leaders is severely limited if the tenure, pay, and promotion prospects of public administrators in office are dependent upon the approval of those leaders. The exercise of meaningful discretion by public administrators makes it desirable that a significant number of administrative appointments be protected from political control so that the pressure that political leaders can exert on individual public administrators is limited. A career civil service then, by providing such protection, increases the discretion available to public administrators in following the directives of political leaders.

Problem of agency! [handwritten note in right margin]

The importance of the career service in insulating public administration from political influence has, of course, long been recognized in the field of American public administration. Frank Goodnow (1900) believed that the survival of popular government depended "largely on our ability to prevent politics from exercising too great an influence over administration, and the parties in control of the administration from using it to influence improperly the expression of the public will" (132). However, Goodnow and others saw a career service primarily as a means of reducing political corruption and improving the competence and efficiency of government, rather than as a general check on political power. Indeed, as suggested in chapter five, these writers held a largely instrumentalist vision of public administration in which the notion of administration as a check on power would seem unacceptable. What they did not fully appreciate was that a career service in limiting the corrupting influences of politics must also inevitably reduce more generally the control that political leaders can exercise over the actions of public administrators.

Moreover, even a merit service can be manipulated [handwritten note]

MODERN WRITINGS ON ADMINISTRATION
AS A CHECK ON POWER

Given the strong influence of rationalism on public administration, it is perhaps not surprising that the idea of administration as a check on power has not been widely articulated by public administration writers. The idea has, however, received some support. Vincent Ostrom (1979), for example, despite his sharp critique of bureaucratic structures and processes, has suggested that public administrators should play a role in checking the power of political leaders. According to Ostrom (1979):

> The public servant in a democratic society is not the neutral and obedient servant to his master's command. He will refuse to obey unlawful efforts to exploit the common wealth or to use the coercive capabilities

of the state to impair the rights of persons, but he will use reason and peaceful persuasion in taking such stands (131).

George Frederickson and David Hart (1985) seem to go further in arguing that public administrators have a duty to uphold the regime values of their nation and to resist the oppressive policies of their political leaders. Frederickson and Hart discuss with admiration the resistance of Danish civil servants to their Nazi leaders during the German occupation in World War II and point to it as an example of the type of administrative heroism they would like to see in the United States. They recount the efforts of Danish civil servants in protecting the rights of the Jews:

> They found finances, guaranteed the sanctity of Jewish homes and properties, protected Jewish funds, and performed innumerable other responsibilities. For the small number of Jews who were captured in the round-up, the Danish government provided oversight. The bureaucracy watched after them in the concentration camp at Theresienstadt, eventually assisting in their release and transfer to Sweden (548).

Frederickson and Hart (1985) note the contrast between public administration in Denmark and public administration in Germany where "the actions of bureaucracy were distinguished by an obsession with career success, which abetted monstrous evil" (549). What is important here is that they see the example of the actions of Danish civil servants as relevant to American public administration. They ask, for example, "but would there not have been real drama if American local government officials had simply refused to discriminate against black people in the 1950s" (549). In other words, Frederickson and Hart see an important role for public administration as a check on power.

Frederickson and Hart's vision of public administration is perhaps more radical than the anti-rationalist approach suggested here. It seems sometimes perhaps supportive even of actions taken by administrators outside the law. However, their notion of administrative discretion as a check on the abuse of political power is consistent with an anti-rationalist vision of public administration. Furthermore, the events of the Watergate and the Iran-Contra affairs illustrate clearly the relevance of their arguments within the American context. Indeed, it is interesting to recall here that two of the heroes of the Watergate affair were Elliot Richardson and William Ruckelshaus, both of whom were dismissed for resisting President Nixon's order to fire special prosecutor Archibald Cox.

THE ANGLO-AMERICAN TRADITION
OF ADMINISTRATIVE DISCRETION

The idea of using administrative discretion to check power is also not without historical precedent. Up until the nineteenth century, local administrative authorities in Britain enjoyed considerable independence in the enforcement of laws passed by Parliament (Goodnow 1900). There was an understanding that the concurrence of local authorities was necessary to the execution of laws passed by Parliament. This was a reaction to earlier abuses of power by the Crown and, according to Frank Goodnow (1900), "It was due to this system that the Stuarts were unable to establish the system of absolute government for which they struggled so desperately and so long" (43).

In other words, in response to exploitative sovereigns, there evolved a tradition in Britain of using administrative discretion as a device to limit political power. The British system of local government was to a considerable degree adopted by the American states in establishing the relationships between state governments and local elected officials. These local officials, including county commissioners, sheriffs, and school board officials, even today continue to exercise significant independence in administering state policies. Furthermore, there are numerous examples in our history where, even if public administration is not explicitly seen as a check on power, it has nonetheless been deliberately insulated from the direct influence of elected political officials in such a way that public administrators can act independently of the particular desires of those officials (Cook 1992). Examples here include independent public authorities, regulatory commissions, and the Federal Reserve Board.

The importance of the role of public administration in checking power in American political tradition is confirmed by the observations of Alexis de Tocqueville (1969), who studied the workings of American government and society in the early part of the nineteenth century. Tocqueville believed that decentralized administration was important in the United States as a means of checking the tyranny of the majority. Consistent with an anti-rationalist perspective, he was concerned about the potential abuse of majority power. Tocqueville (1969) argued that the democratization of government in the United States had made "the power of the majority not only predominant but irresistible" (247) and that, once the majority has made its mind up, there are "no obstacles which can retard, much less halt, its progress and give it time to hear the wails of those it crushes as it passes" (248). He believed that this centralized political power of the majority in the United States, if combined with centralized administrative power, would lead to "a republic despotism . . .

more intolerable than in any of the absolute monarchies of Europe" (263). As Tocqueville observed:

> If the directing power in American societies had both these means of government at its disposal and combined the right to command with the faculty and habit to perform everything itself, if having established the general principles of the government, it entered into the details of their application, and having regulated the great interests of the country, it came down to consider even individual interests, then freedom would soon be banished from the New World (262).

Fortunately, in Tocqueville's view, what tempered the tyranny of the majority in the United States was the absence of administrative centralization. He noted that "in the United States, the majority, though it often has a despot's tastes and instincts, still lacks the most improved instruments of tyranny" (Tocqueville 1969, 262). He argued that "the sovereign commands of its representative, the central government, have to be carried out by agents who often do not depend upon it and cannot be given directions every minute" (262–263). According to Tocqueville, the municipal bodies and counties, which formed the basis for public administration at that time, were "like so many hidden reefs retarding or dividing the flood of the popular will" and that, as a result, "if the law were oppressive, liberty would still find some shelter from the way the law is carried into execution" (263). In short then, public administration in the United States was seen by Tocqueville as checking the discretionary power of political leaders.

The use of administrative discretion as a check on power is, therefore, an important part of our Anglo-American political tradition. It is an aspect of our political tradition, however, which public administration writers have generally overlooked; the exception here being Goodnow who was clearly critical of it. That this aspect of American political tradition has been slighted by public administration writers, however, should not be surprising. Early public administration writers were strongly influenced in their writings by European rather than by English or American traditions of administration. Woodrow Wilson (1955), for example, made explicit his lack of concern for that part of the Anglo-American political tradition that related to public administration when he argued that, in studying administration:

> We can never learn either our own weaknesses or our own virtues by comparing ourselves with ourselves . . . Perhaps even the English system is too much like our own to be used to the most profit in illustra-

tion. It is best on the whole to get entirely away from our own atmosphere and be most careful in examining such systems as those of France and Germany (21).

Wilson sought to "Americanize" the science of administration as "developed by French and German professors" (7). However, by relying so heavily on Continental traditions of administration, he and other early public administration writers were perhaps led to ignore a key aspect of Anglo-American political tradition, namely the tradition of administration as a check on political power.

CHECKING ADMINISTRATIVE POWER:
RULES AND PROCEDURES

While administrative discretion has value in checking the power of political leaders, there is also a need, from an anti-rationalist perspective, to check the discretionary power of public administrators. Public administrators are, after all, no less fallible as human beings than are elected leaders. John Rohr (1986) has argued that the moral and ethical character of public administrators should be relied upon to restrain the abuse of administrative discretion. His argument in this respect is similar to that of discretionists like Carl Friedrich who wish to rely on the moral "inner checks" of public administrators to check administrative abuse of power. However, as indicated in chapter five, the "inner checks" provided by the values of public administrators, while important, should not be seen as adequate alone to check their power. In this respect, an anti-rationalist perspective on public administration would suggest the need for a greater concern than that expressed by Rohr regarding the abuse of administrative discretion. As James Madison noted, "Enlightened statesmen will not always be at the helm" (Wills 182, 45). From an anti-rationalist perspective then, the exercise of administrative discretion must itself be subject to limits beyond those of ethics.

In particular, the discretionary power exercised by public administrators can and should be constrained by the development of bureaucratic rules and procedures that limit their discretion, while maintaining their independence from political leaders. For example, where public administrators have discretion over expenditures, such rules and procedures may include legally binding limits on expenditures, detailed line-item budgets and expenditure reports, encumbrance accounting, and central review of major purchase requests and contracts. Also, the ability of public administrators to hire or fire subordinates should be limited. Of course, to have an effect on administrative behavior, rules and procedures must be enforced. This requires the development of hierarchical structures to monitor compliance and a system of rewards and sanctions so that public administrators are motivated to comply with rules and procedures. Also, regular audits are necessary as an external check on compliance.

The notion that bureaucratic rules and procedures are important in checking the power of public administrators is consistent with Herbert Kaufman's analysis of "red tape." As Kaufman notes (1977), while many bemoan the existence of red tape in public agencies, it is a price we pay for keeping government "from turning into an instrumentality of private profit for those in its employ or those with private fortunes at their disposal" (50). Without "exceedingly tight" financial controls, for example, public monies would be "diverted from their intended uses to the enrichment of dishonest public servants" (51).

Also important here, from an anti-rationalist perspective, are administrative rules that limit the ability of public administrators to treat citizens in an arbitrary and discriminatory fashion. Some discretion in the treatment of citizens is obviously inevitable, particularly given the redistributive nature of modern government. However, public administrators should not feel free to treat each case on its merits, but rather ought, wherever possible, to be able to justify their actions, particularly their coercive actions, in terms of general rules applicable to all. John Locke (1939b) saw this when he argued that "freedom of men under government is to have a standing rule to live by, common to everyone of that society" and "not to be subject to the inconstant, uncertain, unknown, arbitrary will of another man" (412). In the absence of such rules, administrators, as fallible human beings guided only by limited reason and flawed motives, may be more likely to undertake acts that arbitrarily favor some citizens and penalize others. The exercise of arbitrary discrimination between citizens in this fashion is no less to be guarded against than the abuse of majority power. David Hume (1984) was clearly aware of the importance of general rules applicable to all in limiting human discretion more broadly when he observed that:

> Were men . . . to take the liberty of acting with regard to the laws of society, as they do in every other affair, they wou'd conduct themselves, on most occasions, by particular judgements, and wou'd take into consideration the characters and circumstances of the persons, as well as the general nature of the question. But 'tis easy to observe . . . that the avidity and partiality of men wou'd quickly bring disorder into the world, if not restrain'd by some general and inflexible principles. 'Twas

therefore, with a view to this inconvenience, that men have establish'd those principles, and have agreed to restrain themselves by general rules, which are unchangeable by spite and favor, and by particular views or private and public interest (584).

General rules providing for the equal treatment of citizens under the law provide then a necessary check on the abuse of administrative discretion. The development of rules consistent with equal treatment of citizens is admittedly not always easy. Rules inevitably classify individuals and groups within the group of citizens. However, from an anti-rationalist perspective, rules, if they are to effectively check administrative discretion, should not be used with the deliberate intent of conveying benefits to or imposing costs on particular individuals. This requires that they be cast in terms sufficiently general that the individuals who gain or lose from them should not be identifiable. As Friedrich Hayek (1960) argued, "The ideal of equality of law is aimed at equally improving the chances of yet unknown people but incompatible with benefiting or harming individuals in a predictable manner" (210).

This idea that public administrators should not be free to discriminate in how they treat citizens but rather should be bound by rules providing for equality of treatment may seem, at first glance, incompatible with the exercise of significant administrative discretion. However, there is no reason, from an anti-rationalist perspective, why administrative agencies themselves rather than legislators should not take the lead and be required to develop such rules. It is not so important here who draws up the rules as that they should be drawn up by somebody, and that they should be applicable to all. As Hayek (1944) observed, "so long as the power that is delegated is merely the power to make general rules, there may be very good reasons why such rules should be laid down by local rather than by the central authority" (66). Hayek (1960) further argued that rules "drawn up by the administrative authority itself but duly published in advance and strictly adhered to will be more in conformity with the rule of law than will vague discretionary powers conferred on the administrative organs by legislative action" (226). The anti-rationalist argument for the use of rules to limit arbitrary discretion need not, therefore, rule out an active role for public administrators in shaping public policy. Through the writing of appropriate general administrative rules, public administrators can still exercise significant discretion in the implementation of public policies.

Obviously, rules providing for the equal treatment of citizens must be enforced if they are to be effective so that hierarchical control is again necessary here. Also important, however, is the availability to citizens of avenues of

But all of this will require t discuhn
So how available as a check? Ultimately
have to rely on internal controls?

appeal against administrative rulings. These include the right to an impartial administrative hearing as well as the right to appeal administrative decisions to courts of law. Such avenues of appeal are necessary if citizens are to be able to protect themselves against arbitrary administrative actions. They are also important in providing administrators with knowledge regarding gaps or ambiguities in rules and in bringing to light unforeseen consequences of rules.

The importance of rules and procedures as a check on arbitrary administrative actions has been emphasized by Kenneth Culp Davis (1969). Davis shows vividly how the absence of administrative rules in such diverse areas as traffic enforcement, criminal prosecution, public housing, industrial regulation, and public welfare assistance can lead to the arbitrary treatment of citizens by administrators. He sees administrative rule making rather than legislative direction as the chief instrument for confining administrative discretion. According to Davis (1969), "The typical failure in our system that is correctible . . . is the procrastination of administrators in resorting to the rule-making power to replace vagueness with clarity" (56–57). Davis argues that "administrators must strive to do as much as they reasonably can to develop and to make known the needed confinements of discretionary power through standards, principles, and rules" (59).

It should be emphasized here that the purpose of administrative rules and procedures in an anti-rationalist public administration is not to force public administrators to follow the directives of political leaders more closely. Rather their purpose is to limit the abuse of power by public administrators either for self-interested or other ends. The concern over administrative discretion expressed here, therefore, is not the same as that expressed by political scientists such as Theodore Lowi (1979), who seek to use rules as a means of strengthening administrative accountability to elected leaders. Indeed, from an anti-rationalist perspective, the types of rules limiting administrative discretion, which Lowi advocates, might be harmful in increasing the ability of political leaders to control public administrators and hence their ability to exploit citizens.

CHECKING ADMINISTRATIVE POWER: CITIZEN PARTICIPATION

Citizen participation in the administrative decision-making process in the form of providing information, advice, and opinions to public administrators can also play an important role from an anti-rationalist perspective in checking administrative discretion. Citizen participation can be particularly helpful

in providing the professional administrator with practical knowledge, possessed by citizens, concerning the effects of administrative decisions on them.
By doing this, citizen participation makes it more likely that the harmful
effects of administrative decisions on citizens will be considered in the administrative process. While such knowledge obviously cannot necessarily force
public administrators to modify their decisions, it may at least prevent public
administrators from inadvertently exploiting citizens because of lack of
knowledge. Given the limits of reason and the inevitable existence of uncertainty facing administrators, this type of check on administrative discretion is
not without importance. Citizen participation also provides a means of
informing citizens about particular administrative actions and their possible
effects so that they are better able to protect their interests in the political process. In this way, citizen participation can check administrative discretion in
an indirect fashion by encouraging citizens to enlist the support of political
leaders to help protect them against administrative abuse.

It must be recognized here, of course, that citizen participation may
sometimes increase the risk of exploitative policies by increasing the power
that particular groups of citizens can exercise over others in administrative
decision making. Such influence may result in administrative decisions that
benefit these groups at the expense of others. Citizen representatives are, after
all, also fallible human beings and can be expected sometimes to pursue their
own interests or passions without regard to the costs imposed on their fellow
citizens. The problem of co-optation of administrative bodies by particular
groups of citizens for their own purposes is well known (Selznick 1949). The
need to check undue influence by particular groups on administrative decisions would indicate that the process of citizen participation must itself be
governed by rules and procedures. These should provide for a broad representation of interests and viewpoints and an open decision-making process, and
should make explicit how the interests and viewpoints of various groups are
to be considered in making administrative decisions.

Furthermore, consistent with the discussion above, the discretion exercised by administrators in responding to citizen input must itself be
restrained by general rules providing, to the extent possible, for equal treatment of citizens. Requiring public administrators to formulate their
responses to citizen input or recommendations in the form of general rules
rather than particular arbitrary actions can be helpful here because such rules
make it more difficult for public administrators to take actions that reward or
penalize particular individuals or groups. While not without some risk then,
the process of citizen participation can be structured in such a fashion that it
contributes to the checking of power.

*None of this works, in the way
the rep. of pum schm does, because
adm doesn't possess any nd. source
of legitimacy and authority.*

INERTIA, INFLEXIBILITY AND IMPERSONALITY

An anti-rationalist public administration then is one that possesses substantial discretion in following the directives of political leaders but is restrained in the exercise of its discretion, at the same time, by an extensive system of rules and procedures and by broad citizen participation. This analysis has certain implications for the general character of an anti-rationalist bureaucracy. Firstly, at least as perceived by political leaders and their supporters, an anti-rationalist bureaucracy may sometimes display a certain degree of inertia or a lack of responsiveness to the policy innovations of political leaders. It may sometimes respond only slowly and with some resistance to attempts to change policy directions. Such inertia is inevitable when public administrators are able to exercise discretion in following the directives of political leaders. Bureaucratic inertia is also likely be accentuated by the existence of administrative rules and procedures and the need to involve a broad spectrum of citizens in the administrative decision-making process.

Secondly, at least as perceived by those who work within it, an anti-rationalist bureaucracy will seem inflexible and oriented more to compliance with rules and procedures than to the achievement of results. Its rules for budgets, personnel, and procurement will sometimes seem frustrating for administrators who wish to make administrative changes that they believe rightly or wrongly are beneficial to citizens. This inflexibility is an inevitable consequence of rules and procedures designed to limit dishonest and arbitrary actions by public administrators. Thirdly, at least as perceived by citizens who deal with it, an anti-rationalist bureaucracy will seem impersonal and often unwilling to take into account individual circumstances and needs in making decisions affecting citizens. This impersonality is to be expected when administrators are restrained by general rules providing for equal treatment of citizens.

What is perhaps ironic here then is that an anti-rationalist bureaucracy can be expected to reflect characteristics that are commonly thought of as "defects" of bureaucracy: inertia, inflexibility, and impersonality (Downs 1967). Such defects are to a considerable extent unavoidable if public administrators are to serve as a check on political power and, at the same time, be restrained from exploiting citizens. Max Weber (1947) saw this in regard to the impersonality of bureaucracy when he observed that a general consequence of bureaucracy is:

The dominance of a spirit of formalistic impersonality, 'Sine ira et studio', without hatred or passion, and hence without affection or enthusiasm . . . Everyone is subject to formal equality of treatment; that is, everyone in the same empirical situation. This is the spirit in which the ideal official conducts his office (340).

This is not to deny that the inertia, inflexibility, and impersonality displayed by public bureaucracies may on occasion be excessive, but rather simply to point out that an overly responsive, flexible, and personal bureaucracy carries with it significant risks for the welfare of citizens. A bureaucracy that is overly responsive to the wishes of political leaders risks becoming an instrument of exploitation for political leaders. A bureaucracy that is overly flexible in its operations and overly personal in its dealings with citizens risks becoming a source of exploitation itself.

CONSTRAINED DISCRETION

What an anti-rationalist perspective suggests then is a system of what might be termed "constrained discretion." According to this approach, the power of political leaders to exploit citizens should be checked by providing public administrators with significant discretion within the law in following the directives of political leaders. At the same time, however, administrative discretion should be itself checked by a system of administrative rules and procedures. These rules and procedures should limit the ability of public administrators to enrich themselves at the expense of the public and should limit arbitrary actions taken against citizens. Administrative discretion should further be checked by a process of citizen participation structured to provide administrators with knowledge about the effects of their decisions from a broad array of interests and viewpoints.

In this respect, even the very broad type of policy discretion, currently enjoyed for example by independent regulatory commissions, may be seen as supported by an anti-rationalist perspective. Indeed, as both Brian Cook (1992) and Louis Fisher (1987) have argued, the development of independent regulatory commissions is quite consistent with our constitutional tradition in limiting the power that the president can exert over administration. To the extent that there is a problem with the broad discretion exercised by such agencies, it is that this discretion may not, in all cases, be adequately restrained by administrative rules and procedures, thus resulting sometimes in arbitrary administrative actions against citizens (Davis 1969).

The type of system of constrained discretion advocated here recognizes that human fallibility places limits on both the reason of political leaders and the reason of public administrators. It sees public administrators explicitly as part of a constitutional system of checks on the abuse of power. It justifies administrative discretion not on the grounds of any superior powers of reason exercised by administrators, but on the grounds of the necessarily imperfect powers of reason possessed by political leaders, but then, recognizing the imperfections of administrators, it seeks to also check their exercise of reason. As such, a system of constrained discretion then is consistent with the anti-rationalist worldview of the Founders.

7

The Ethics of Administrative Discretion

The foregoing analysis has suggested that a substantial measure of administrative discretion, albeit constrained, is desirable in a constitutional system of government designed to check power. The question arises then as to <u>what normative principles should guide the exercise of administrative discretion</u>. While, as indicated in chapter five, ethical principles alone cannot provide an adequate check on power, this does not mean that they are unimportant. None of us would be comfortable with a bureaucracy populated largely by amoral or immoral public administrators.

ANTI-RATIONALISM AND ETHICS

Certainly, an anti-rationalist perspective, despite its emphasis on human fallibility, does not discount the importance of ethical rules. Indeed, it lays great emphasis on habits and customs, as well as formal rules, in restraining the destructive impulses of individuals and in protecting the social order. Despite David Hume's (1987) emphasis on the role of private interests and passions in public affairs, he argued that "general virtue and good morals in a state" are "requisite to happiness" (55). Adam Smith (1982) also demonstrated his belief in the importance of ethics when he argued that "he is not a citizen who is not disposed to respect the laws and to obey the civil magistrate; and he is certainly not a good citizen who does not wish to promote, by every means in his power, the welfare of the whole society of his fellow-citizens" (231).

The importance of ethical behavior was also appreciated by the Founders, who by no means dispensed with the concept of virtue in their writings. They believed that citizens and public officials could and should exhibit virtue. The Founders saw their constitutional checks on power as necessary but by no means sufficient to provide good government. Virtue was also required for a healthy republic. James Madison argued that:

> As there is a degree of depravity in mankind which requires a certain degree of circumspection and distrust: So there are other qualities in human nature, which justify a certain portion of esteem and confidence

. . . Were the pictures which have been drawn by the political jealousy of some among us, faithful likenesses of the human character, the inference would be that there is not sufficient virtue among men for self-government; and that nothing less than the chains of despotism can restrain them from destroying and devouring one another (Wills 1982, 284).

At the Virginia ratifying convention, Madison observed that "To suppose that any form of government will secure liberty or happiness without any virtue in the people is a chimerical idea" (Wills 1982, *xxi*). Alexander Hamilton also, despite his dark view of human nature, argued that:

The supposition of universal venality in human nature is little less an error in political reasoning than the supposition of universal rectitude. The institution of delegated power implies that there is a portion of virtue and honor among mankind . . . It has been found to exist in the most corrupt periods of the most corrupt governments (Wills 1982, 387).

Ethical principles are, therefore, by no means irrelevant to an anti-rationalist vision of government and public administration. Furthermore, the anti-rationalist perspective does provide at least some insight into what types of ethical principles might be desirable or undesirable. It is useful to begin here by discussing what is perhaps the least controversial rule, the rule of personal honesty.

PERSONAL HONESTY

By personal honesty, what is meant here is simply refraining from engaging in illegal or corrupt activities. Clearly, from an anti-rationalist perspective, ethical rules should at a minimum constrain public administrators from dishonestly using their discretion to pursue their personal financial interests at the expense of citizens. The diversion of public resources for personal use, the selling of valuable information, or the selling of administrative discretion by administrators all constitute means by which public administrators can exploit citizens. Indeed, as historical experience in Europe and more recent experience in some developing nations confirms, such behavior can result in a government run almost entirely for the private financial benefit of officials without much, if any, regard for the welfare of citizens.

Formal bureaucratic rules and procedures are important here in limiting such corrupt behavior. However, ethical rules can also be helpful in encouraging compliance with such rules and hence also can limit the exploitative aspects of government behavior. Indeed, without some moral sense of honesty on the part of public administrators, the enforcement of bureaucratic rules against dishonest behavior would become very costly if not actually impossible. Furthermore, since formal rules prohibiting dishonest behavior are inevitably imperfect and have gaps or loopholes, which public administrators may sometimes be tempted to use to their personal advantage, ethical rules of honesty can also serve to encourage administrators to conform to, not only the letter of the law, but also the spirit of the law. As Dennis Thompson (1992) has noted, "appearing to do wrong while doing right is really doing wrong" (257).

The importance of rules prohibiting simple dishonesty seems to have been deemphasized in much of the writing on public administration ethics. John Rohr (1978), for example, has termed this approach somewhat disparagingly the "low road" approach to ethics. Rohr sees an emphasis on compliance with these sorts of ethical rules as "hopelessly negative" and trivial (54). It is true, of course, that ethical behavior on the part of public administrators requires more than simple honesty. Nonetheless, from an anti-rationalist perspective, compliance with such rules must be seen as a fundamental component of administrative ethics.

In light of the fallible nature of public administrators as human beings, the temptation to misuse public office for personal financial gain is by no means negligible. If public administrators come to see rules providing for simple honesty as trivial and act accordingly, then the likelihood increases that citizens will come to see public administration as a source of exploitation rather than a source of value. Certainly, the stories of local and state government corruption to be found in many local newspapers in the United States do little to raise the regard in which public service is held at the local and state level. Similarly, revelations about corruption in the Department of Justice and the Department of Housing and Urban Development in the 1980s may well have contributed to the lack of legitimacy of government at the federal level.

Ethical rules providing for personal honesty, therefore, are important and warrant perhaps more emphasis in the literature than they have been accorded. What other principles should be important in guiding administrative discretion from an anti-rationalist perspective? It may be useful to begin by exploring three different approaches to administrative ethics that are commonly discussed by public administration writers: neutrality, utility, and social equity.

NEUTRALITY

Neutrality is the traditional public administration ethic. An ethical rule of neutrality is implicit in the politics-administration dichotomy emphasized by early writers. The idea here is that public administrators should conscientiously avoid allowing their political beliefs to affect their administrative actions and should carry out the instructions of their political leaders in the most efficient and effective manner. This ethical principle of administrative action is based on the instrumentalist view of public administration, advocated by Herman Finer (1941) and discussed earlier in chapter five. According to this view, public administration should be a neutral instrument of the political will of a community as expressed through its elected leaders. Where administrative discretion exists, because of vagueness or gaps in legislation, the ethical principle of neutrality would suggest that public administrators should seek to determine what elected leaders intend or would intend the administrator to do in a particular situation. This is what John Burke (1986) seems to have in mind when he argues that bureaucratic responsibility entails first that "officials have a basic duty, other things being equal, to take the dictates of higher authorities seriously" (39).

Burke's advice to take the dictates of democratically elected officials seriously has its obvious merits. As indicated in the last chapter, nobody would seriously advocate that public administrators should feel free to ignore the specific lawful directives of elected leaders. Such advice to administrators would be an invitation to bureaucratic tyranny. However, the notion that, in the absence of clear direction, administrators should ascertain and then act according to the intentions of elected leaders is problematic. This is because it urges upon administrators a purely instrumentalist view of their responsibilities. As we have seen in chapter five, the instrumentalist view of public administration raises serious concerns about unchecked electoral power from an anti-rationalist perspective. Simply implementing the wishes of political leaders on each and every matter runs the risk of rendering public administration an instrument for the exploitation of citizens. The ethical rule of neutrality would facilitate such exploitation by strengthening the control of political leaders over the administrative process and would seem, therefore, to be inconsistent with an anti-rationalist perspective. As Norton Long (1993) has argued, in discussing administrative ethics:

Those who argue for . . . a narrow instrumentalist view of the appropriate role of the bureaucracy and . . . the abject subservience of civil servants to ministers, should consider carefully the costs entailed and whether they are really prepared to accept those costs. The temptations to politicize an agency to use its powers in a narrowly partisan manner and to manage information in order to manipulate public opinion are strong and real (7).

Furthermore, even if we suppose that public administrators should seek to follow the intentions of political leaders, it is often far from clear whose intentions they should follow. Political leaders, after all, as representatives of all of us, have multiple and conflicting interests and objectives, and, while supporting a particular program or policy, they may disagree as to how such a program or policy should be implemented at the administrative level. Where legislation is not clear and administrative discretion exists, such discretion often exists precisely because the political leaders supporting it could not agree on all issues. The passage of legislation at the federal level requires, after all, both negotiations between and the assent of several hundred legislators and the president. It would be surprising if many of them did not hold somewhat different views as to how public administrators should act in particular situations. If this is the case, then whose intentions should guide the administrator? The principle of ethical neutrality provides little guidance to the administrator in choosing among competing interpretations of legislation provided by different political leaders.

Finally, given the limits of reason, it is not likely that the legislature would or even could anticipate all of the particular situations in which public administrators might apply the law. In fact, the role of public administrators consists, in significant part, in using their own expertise and experience to determine how the law should be applied in particular unforeseen situations. Political leaders may not have well-formed opinions in many cases as to how the public administrator should act in a particular situation. They may expect administrators to exercise their own judgment. This is particularly true where actions require a specialized competence. In these situations, the rule of ethical neutrality again can provide only limited guidance.

If public administrators were to act according to the ethical rule of neutrality they would still then, in many cases, possess significant discretion with little ethical guidance as to how to exercise it. In these cases, the rule of neutrality will provide little check on the exercise of discretionary power by public administrators. From an anti-rationalist perspective, therefore, the rule of neutrality does not adequately address the problem of the abuse of power by either political leaders or public administrators.

UTILITY

The utilitarian approach to ethics would suggest that public administrators should use their discretion so as to maximize the happiness of the greatest number of individuals. Administrative choices, according to the principle of utility, should not be evaluated against abstract a priori values such as equity or liberty, but rather should be assessed in terms of their real consequences for the happiness of all individuals in society. Perhaps not surprisingly, given its pragmatic emphasis on evaluating the consequences of actions, the utilitarian approach has had considerable appeal for public administration writers.

Dwight Waldo (1984) has argued that the early public administration movement and utilitarianism were "closely similar in temper, in motives, in philosophic presumptions" (79). Marshall Dimock (1936), for example, appeared to advocate a distinctly utilitarian approach when he urged that administrators in assessing their actions should go beyond a "mechanical concept" of efficiency and should embrace a "social and long-range view of efficiency" that "encompasses all the persons and results involved in operating an individual enterprise" (123). The utilitarian emphasis is also clear in the more recent writings of policy analysts, such as Charles Schultze (1968), who seek to strengthen the role of techniques of cost-benefit and cost-effectiveness analysis in the public decision-making process. These analytic techniques are rooted in welfare economics, which typically takes utility-maximization as the major guide for normative analysis (Haveman and Margolis 1983).

Utilitarian approaches undoubtedly have some merit. Nobody would suggest that administrators should not attempt to think about the benefits and costs of their actions to others. Cost-benefit analysis and cost-effectiveness analysis can be useful in forcing public administrators to engage in systematic thinking about the consequences of their actions. However, utilitarianism, as noted in chapter two, is an essentially rationalist doctrine. Not surprisingly then, it raises concerns from an anti-rationalist perspective. Firstly, it presumes a great deal in terms of our ability to evaluate the consequences of our actions for the happiness of individuals. As Friedrich Hayek (1976) has argued, utilitarianism "must proceed on a factual assumption of omniscience which is never satisfied in real life" and fails to take account of our "inescapable ignorance of most of the particular circumstances which determine the effects of our actions" (20). Public administrators can rarely foresee, let alone measure, all of the benefits and costs to citizens of alternative choices.

Attempts to measure identifiable outcomes will typically involve making assumptions concerning future events and concerning people's preferences—assumptions about which even reasonable men and women may differ. As a result, utilitarianism may not always provide a clear guide for administrative action and so may not provide an adequate ethical check on the use of administrative discretion.

Secondly, a utilitarian approach assumes that, for purposes of ethical analysis, conflicting interests and preferences can somehow be reconciled by simply adding up or otherwise aggregating individual utilities into some single whole. Under such conditions, any government action can be rationalized so long as the costs incurred by those citizens who lose from it are more than offset by the benefits enjoyed by other citizens who gain. Like majority rule, utilitarianism then does not prevent exploitation of citizens by government, but only changes its form. Instead of exploitation by the majority, utilitarianism risks exploitation by those whose utility gains from government actions exceed the utility losses of others. For example, if racist attitudes are held with sufficient intensity among a sufficient number of citizens, then racist actions on the part of administrators can be justified on utilitarian grounds.

This is not to deny that a utilitarian approach, by taking account of the intensity of citizen preferences, might provide a better protection for minorities in some instances than would be provided by simple majority rule. It is rather simply to suggest that following a utilitarian approach need not rule out policies that impose severe costs on some citizens. From an anti-rationalist perspective then, utilitarianism cannot be seen as providing an adequate check on administrative discretion and could provide, in fact, a rationale for exploitation.

SOCIAL EQUITY

Since the early 1970s, there has been much discussion in the public administration literature about social equity as an ethical principle for public administrators. The New Public Administration took social equity as its central organizing principle (Frederickson 1971). However, what is meant by social equity is not always clear. As George Frederickson (1990) has noted, social equity can have a variety of meanings. If, by social equity, what is meant is equality before the law then this poses little problem from an anti-rationalist perspective. Indeed, an ethical rule encouraging public administrators to treat citizens in an equal and impartial fashion would be helpful in limiting the arbitrary exercise of discretion. Furthermore, to the extent that a concern with social equity might lead public administrators to try and limit the harm that government actions would impose upon citizens, this would also be consistent with an anti-rationalist perspective. However, it seems that many public administration writers either do not mean this or that they mean considerably more than this.

Specifically, as noted in chapter five, supporters of the New Public Administration argue that public administrators should seek to enhance the political and economic power of disadvantaged minorities (Frederickson 1971). David Hart (1974), for example, argues that "the equitable public administrator has both the duty and the obligation to deploy his efforts on behalf of the less advantaged" (9). Public administrators are to engage themselves then in a racial and class struggle in society on behalf of particular groups.

This notion that public administrators should feel either ethically empowered or ethically bound to use their discretion to actively seek a particular outcome in terms of the distribution of wealth and power in a society is troubling from an anti-rationalist perspective. The anti-rationalist perspective would suggest that public administrators should protect all citizens, even those who are not seen as disadvantaged, from the exploitative actions of government. In contrast, the social equity perspective suggests that they should become the permanent self-designated agents of the interests of particular groups or classes in society. Also, it suggests that these public administrators should use the coercive powers of government on behalf of these groups, even where it is at the expense of other citizens. Such a strategy clearly runs the risk of having public administrators use their discretion to engage in actions that have exploitative consequences. Victor Thompson (1975), a critic of the New Public Administration, sees this when he argues that it "is a call for equity by means of 'theft' and 'subversion' on the basis of the ageless fallacy that the end justifies the means" (11).

Furthermore, it is far from clear what particular distributional outcome public administrators should strive for. Given the limits of reason and differing and conflicting interests and views among individuals, there would seem to be no ideal or uniquely just distribution of wealth or power in society that can be determined or agreed upon. Most of us would probably agree that some assistance should be provided to the poor or disadvantaged. However, precisely who is disadvantaged, how much assistance should be provided, and how that assistance should be provided is not at all clear. Reason alone cannot determine unambiguously who really are the disadvantaged in society and what precisely should be done to promote their interests. Hayek (1944) stated clearly the problem facing government when it seeks to use its power to obtain some supposedly just distribution of wealth or income:

But how can and how will [government] use that power? By what principles will it or ought it to be guided? Is there a definite answer to the innumerable questions of relative merits that will arise and that will have to be solved deliberately? Is there a scale of values, on which reasonable people can be expected to agree, which would justify a new hierarchical order of society and is likely to satisfy the demands for justice? (109)

From an anti-rationalist perspective, there is no agreed upon social welfare function that defines a desirable distribution of income or wealth, or that prescribes appropriate redistributive actions for either political leaders or public administrators. These are issues about which, given the limits of reason, even reasonable men and women may disagree and may disagree quite strongly. One suspects that there are considerable disagreements even among those who argue for the criterion of social equity. As Madison noted, "the most common and durable source of factions, has been the various and unequal distribution of property" (Wills 1982, 44). Because of this ambiguity and conflict concerning the meaning of social equity, while it may provide sentimental gratification to those public administrators of a more egalitarian bent, social equity would seem to be unable to provide an operational guide for ethical decision making.

To suggest, therefore, that, in the absence of any sort of clear prescription or agreement on these issues in society, public administrators should use their discretion consistently to promote the interests of a particular group or faction of citizens in society may well be conducive to actions that are both arbitrary and potentially exploitative of citizens in general. Far from contributing to the constitutional checking of power, a social equity approach would seem to invite the misuse of power, by encouraging public administrators to use their own personal visions of social justice as a rationale for actively imposing costs on those with whom they do not sympathize. Certainly, in an era of ideological dissensus, such an activist egalitarian role for public administrators would be likely to increase social conflict substantially and would earn them little in the way of legitimacy from citizens as a whole.

COMMON-LAW REASONING

From an anti-rationalist perspective, the rules of neutrality, utility, and social equity do not seem to provide adequate criteria for the exercise of administrative discretion. None of them serve to alleviate anti-rationalist concerns about the need to check the exercise of discretionary power by both political leaders and administrators. Consistent with the idea of constrained discretion, what is required is an ethical approach that limits the arbitrary use of discretion by administrators while permitting them to serve a role in checking the power of political leaders. What this suggests, in my view, is that administrators might perhaps seek to develop an ethical basis for action by using common-law reasoning in the exercise of administrative discretion.

Common law, of course, is law based upon precedent. Judges, in applying the common law, seek to find from past decisions, principles or rules that can guide their own decisions. Common-law reasoning or case-law reasoning is reasoning by example. It involves, as Edward Levi (1949) has noted, "a three-step process . . . in which a proposition descriptive of the first case is made into a rule of law and then applied to a next similar situation" (1–2). According to Levi, "The steps are these: similarity is seen between cases; next the rule of law inherent in the first case is announced; then the rule of law is made applicable to the second case" (3).

Levi emphasizes the fact that this type of legal reasoning does not involve the application of fixed rules to particular situations, since judges are bound by the actions of past judges, but not by their past words. He argues that "the determination of similarity or difference" between cases, therefore, "is the function of each judge" (Levi 1949, 2). Each judge, while constrained to seek precedent for his or her actions in the actions of the past, has some freedom to determine what rule is applicable, depending upon what similarities and differences he or she sees as relevant in comparing different cases. Each judge then in looking at a decision in a past case may develop his or her own rule or rationale for that decision and then use that rationale to support a decision in a current case. Legal reasoning here, as Levi notes, "is one in which the classification changes as the classification is made" (3). While, therefore, it must be rooted in the past to a significant extent, common-law reasoning is also a creative process in which the past is reinterpreted from the perspective of the present. This is important for it affords an adaptive character to common law that allows the law to change according to changing social views while still requiring some consistency over time.

The use of common-law reasoning in public administration entails looking for past precedents for alternative actions rather than trying to predict and evaluate the effects of those actions. Public administrators, when guided by common-law reasoning, look to their past actions and the actions of past administrators, determine some type of a rationale for those actions, and then use that rationale to guide their current actions. The applicability of common-law reasoning to the exercise of administrative discretion has been noted by Jay White. According to White (1990):

Administrators are in the same place as lawyers and judges. They . . . employ reasoning by example . . . to determine what ends should be sought and what actions should be taken. Like lawyers and judges they are in the business of making choices about what is true or false, good or bad. Experience suggests this is done on the basis of reasoning by example. Since administrators and judges (or lawyers) are human beings, there is no a priori reason to believe that their reasoning processes are any different: only the contexts differ (138).

Long (1993) also seems to see at least the general relevance of a common-law approach to administrative discretion when he argues that "the development and use of a standard of the public interest by which policies may be evaluated is a high-priority task that can only be effectively undertaken in the same way as the common law, by experience and the cumulative development of standards and by observing the consequences of acting on them" (10). Such an approach, as a basis for the ethical exercise of discretion, is attractive from an anti-rationalist perspective. It yields a number of positive advantages.

Firstly, it reduces uncertainty arising from the exercise of administrative discretion. It permits individuals both inside and outside the bureaucracy, by observing past actions of administrators, to make reasonable, although obviously not certain, predictions about how they will be treated by public administrators in different circumstances. This reduces the costs to others of arbitrary and unpredictable acts of discretion on the part of the administrator. Common-law decision making in general, as Hayek (1973) observed, serves "to tell people which expectations they can count on and which not" (102). Douglass North, a prominent economic historian, likewise argues that common law "provides continuity and essential predictability" (96). To be effective here, of course, administrative decision making must be open and subject to public scrutiny.

Secondly, common-law reasoning provides some degree of consistency or equality in the way in which the cases of individual citizens and employees will be treated by government. Reasoning by example, while it does not eliminate partiality in the treatment of individual cases, at least can restrain it. When engaged in common-law reasoning, administrators are not free to reward or penalize individuals simply as they please but must seek precedents for their actions based on past treatment of individuals. In this way, common- law reasoning can serve as a useful supplement to the use of formal general rules providing for the equal treatment of citizens.

Thirdly, common-law reasoning requires administrators to draw upon the knowledge both explicit and implicit in past decision making, to interpret this in light of current social values and conditions, and then to contribute their own knowledge in the form of precedents for future decisions. It provides the administrator with a frame of reference, based on a current interpretation of past experience, for sorting out what are relevant facts and what are not in a new situation. A system of common-law decision making, as Michael Polanyi (1951) has noted, embodies "the wisdom" with which each consecutive decision "is adjusted to all those made before and to any justified changes in public opinion" (162). As such, like all inheritances, it furnishes what Edmund Burke (1955) referred to as "a sure principle of conservation and a sure principle of transmission without at all excluding a principle of improvement" (38). Common-law decision making provides a link between the knowledge held by past administrators and the knowledge held by current administrators and, in doing so, increases the use of knowledge in the policy process.

Finally, common-law reasoning can assist public administrators in checking the abuse of power by elected leaders. It encourages the administrator to interpret new directives of political leaders in light of past experience and past administrative actions so that there is some continuity between past and present administrative actions. Again, this does not mean that administrators can ignore the specific lawful directives of political leaders. However, by using past administrative practice as the basis for interpreting unclear or ambiguous new directives issued by political leaders, public administrators can exercise a moderating influence over such policies. In this way, they can limit the costs imposed on citizens as a result of innovations or changes in government policies.

Obviously, the common-law approach to administrative discretion is not perfect. It may trap the administrator dealing with new situations into following the bad administrative practices of the past. Administrators, like judges, cannot foresee all of the consequences of the rules or policies that they develop to justify particular decisions. As a result, administrators may sometimes develop rules and policies that, perhaps only later, are seen to have undesirable consequences. These rules and policies may constrain future administrators, who may then be forced to pass on bad precedent to their successors and so on. Administrators, in this fashion, can perpetuate old rules and policies that continue to exploit citizens. Hayek (1973), despite his obvious enthusiasm for judicial common law, conceded that bad precedent is a problem. He argued that the common law may "develop in very undesirable directions" and may require "correction by legislation" (88). Similarly then, administrators may have to announce new administrative rules or policies on occasion that correct the common law, built up by administrative precedent, because of results widely held to be undesirable.

However, notwithstanding the risk of bad precedents, there is still a strong general case for the use of a common-law approach as an ethical basis for the exercise of administrative discretion, particularly when compared with the alternative approaches discussed above. Common-law reasoning provides for some predictability and equity in decision making; it links present knowledge with past knowledge; and it serves to moderate and limit the harmful effects of new policies enacted by political leaders. As such it serves to constrain the discretion of administrators, but still permits them to exercise a constitutional role in using their discretion to check the power of political leaders.

Some will argue that a common-law approach to administrative discretion may slow down changes in public policy and in administrative rules and procedures, because of its tie to past administrative practices, and that, as a result, beneficial outcomes resulting from the more innovative use of administrative discretion may be forgone. This is true to some extent, but an ethical rule based on precedent is no different in this respect from other forms of constitutional rules where, as Alexander Hamilton noted, the prevention of bad laws sometimes entails the failure to enact good laws (Wills 1982, 373–374). Furthermore, as suggested above, common-law reasoning need not eliminate creativity or innovation in administrative decision making. What it asks is that administrators provide a plausible rationale for their actions based upon general rules derived from the past actions of administrators.

That a common-law approach to the exercise of administrative discretion would seem desirable from an anti-rationalist perspective should hardly surprise us. The anti-rationalist worldview, as noted in chapter two, places considerable emphasis on the role of tradition and experience in guiding human action. Common-law reasoning is based in tradition and experience. What has been shown here is that common-law reasoning is also quite consistent with the logic of checking power.

CONSENSUS

Further ethical guidance for public administrators in the exercise of their discretion can be provided by the norm of consensus. Consensus, as a norm for administrative action, is attractive from an anti-rationalist perspective because it serves to limit the costs that public administrators can impose upon citizens as a result of the exercise of their discretion. To the extent that public administrators pursue the norm of consensus, they will be less inclined to take actions that exploit significant minorities. Also, they will be led to interpret the directives of political leaders in a manner that moderates, rather than accentuates, the degree to which citizens are exploited by political leaders. But what is "consensus"?

Consensus is also attractive from an anti-rationalist perspective because it requires that public administrators take account of the knowledge possessed by citizens concerning the effects of public policies. The seeking of consensus, by its very nature, requires that public administrators listen and adjust their positions to a broad array of viewpoints. Finally, in the absence of a definable common good or general will of the community, consensus would seem an appropriate and defensible criterion for administrative action. Indeed, James Buchanan (1979) suggests that "if we reject the notion that there must exist a public or general interest apart from that of the participants, we are necessarily led to the conclusion that only upon unanimous consent of all parties can we be absolutely assured that the total welfare of the group is improved" (153). Given that there will always be differences among individuals as to what constitutes the public good, consensus then may be the best that we can do in evaluating administrative actions.

In order to be meaningful, of course, consensus must be informed. This would suggest that public administrators are obligated, as discussed in chapter six, to provide opportunities for broad citizen participation in making administrative decisions and to provide adequate notice for citizens on upcoming administrative actions. They should not seek consensus simply within a narrow circle of political leaders. Also, public administrators should not mislead political leaders and citizens as to the expected effects of their actions and should be open about the uncertainties surrounding their actions. They should make sure that the different sides of arguments are presented and not simply serve as an advocate of a particular position, however deeply held. This does not rule out administrative advocacy of particular policy decisions, but it does impose a special obligation on administrators to provide a hearing for different perspectives.

Seeking complete consensus or unanimity in decision making is, of course, impractical and, if required, would totally immobilize government. As James Buchanan and Gordon Tullock (1962) have shown, the costs of reaching decisions under a rule of unanimity would be unacceptably high for most public decisions. Nonetheless, from an anti-rationalist perspective, public administrators ought to give substantial weight to seeking decisions that command the broadest feasible support from citizens. Public administrators should seek to avoid polarizing citizens and alienating broad constituencies in the exercise of their discretion. They should consciously seek more than the minimum support required to take administrative actions. They should not permit their zeal for particular courses of action to lead them to neglect the concerns and interests of significant groups of citizens. In short, public administrators should exhibit a preference for consensual solutions to policy problems.

An emphasis on consensual decision making, like common-law reasoning, undoubtedly makes policy change more difficult. It gives strong weight to the interests and preferences in place at a given point in time. However, any proposal for change necessarily must start out from the status quo as an "existential reality" (Buchanan 1975, 78). The desirability of change can only be assessed in comparison to the status quo because that is where we start from. The norm of consensus, like common-law reasoning, need not rule out innovation or creativity. Neither does it restrict the role of the public administrator to one of simply brokering different interests. What an emphasis on the norm of consensus would indicate is rather that public administrators are obliged to look for types of decisions that result in a broad sharing of the benefits and costs of public policies rather than those that simply benefit some citizens at the expense of others. These types of decisions may not always be seen as optimal from the point of either social utility or social equity, but they are more likely to gain support from a consensus.

Furthermore, public administrators should take a role of leadership in advocating and building support for consensual decisions. This can involve not only responding to various individual and group interests but also seeking to persuade them as to where their common interests may lie. It may also involve the packaging of policy proposals in a fashion that minimizes the harm done to particular groups of citizens. Compensation for citizens who bear an undue share of the costs of particular public decisions may be appropriate. Consensual decision making involves a combination of both leadership and deal-making and as such is necessarily a form of politics. However, it should be a politics in which consensus is itself viewed as a desirable end rather than simply a means to some higher purpose.

SUMMARY

We have examined then a number of different approaches to the ethical use of administrative discretion. An anti-rationalist perspective on administrative ethics emphasizes the role of personal honesty but would seem to be in conflict with more ambitious administrative ethics based purely on neutrality, utility, or social equity. Such approaches do not adequately address the problem of checking power. What is argued here is that, given the desirability of checking power in a constitutional system, an approach to administrative discretion based upon both common-law reasoning and consensus may have some merit. An ethical prescription for administrative action, based on precedent and consensus, may strike some here as insufficiently heroic or inspiring for public administrators, but it may be the best available in a world of limited reason, divergent visions of the public good, and fallible human beings. The prescription seems to follow Michael Oakeshott's (1991) advice that a free society "will find its guide in a principle of continuity (which is a diffusion of power between past, present and future) and in a principle of consensus (which is a diffusion of power between the different legitimate interests of the present)" (396).

8
Summary and Conclusion

This book has sought to examine the worldviews or visions of public administration and the Constitution. I have argued that there is a conflict in the worldviews underlying public administration and the Constitution; a conflict between a rationalist worldview, held by most public administration writers, which places great faith in the powers of reason and an anti-rationalist worldview, held by the Founders, which stresses the limits of reason. By embracing, for the most part, the rationalist worldview and rejecting the anti-rationalist worldview of the Founders, public administration writers have made it difficult to argue for the legitimacy of American public administration on constitutional grounds. Obviously, the impact of academic writings on the legitimacy of public administration should not be overstated. However, it is hard to see how public administration can gain much legitimacy when most of those who think, talk, and write about public administration cannot reconcile their thinking with the political tradition that we have inherited from the Founders.

What I have also sought to do here, therefore, is to suggest what a public administration, shaped by an anti-rationalist worldview, might look like. Central to this vision of public administration is the idea, embraced by the Founders, that the discretionary power of government officials, both political leaders and public administrators, should be constrained or checked. Such a vision of public administration rejects the ambitious discretionism of Carl Friedrich, which would grant administrators substantial autonomy but then rely largely on their professional ethics to check administrative abuse. Unchecked administrative discretion is a recipe for administrative tyranny. However, an anti-rationalist vision also rejects the narrow instrumentalism of Herman Finer, which would require strict obedience to the desires of political leaders and would facilitate their abuse of power.

I have argued here that substantial administrative discretion is both necessary and desirable if public administrators are to be able, sometimes, to constrain the ability of political leaders to exploit citizens. I have sought to demonstrate that this is a role that is consistent, not only with the logic of a constitution, but with our own administrative tradition. However, if administrators are not to abuse their power, this discretion must also be constrained.

97

There is a need for rules and procedures aimed at limiting corrupt and arbitrary administrative actions and for a process of citizen participation to inform the exercise of administrative discretion. Furthermore, public administrators need to be guided in the exercise of their discretion by ethical principles that reinforce their constitutional role and limit abuse of power, by requiring that they look conscientiously to precedent and seek consensus in their actions.

THE CONTEMPORARY RELEVANCE
OF THE ANTI-RATIONALIST VISION

This anti-rationalist vision of public administration is consistent with the worldview that shaped the Founders' words and designs. It stands in sharp contrast to the rationalist vision of public administration held by most public administration writers throughout the past century—a vision of public administration as a means of carrying out some general will of the community as interpreted by legislators or administrators. Some might argue that this anti-rationalist vision is based on outmoded ideas; that the emergence of the large activist modern state has superseded the quaint political maxims of this type of eighteenth century Whig philosophy. Not surprisingly, I would disagree.

The growth of the modern state, if anything, would seem to reinforce the importance of the anti-rationalist perspective. Government both commands and generates a larger share of our national income and regulates a wider scope of private action than was true at the time of the Founders. Its functions have extended beyond the provision of basic public goods, like national defense, roads and bridges, and law enforcement, which benefit all citizens, to the provision of selective assistance to particular groups or classes of individuals and to the exercise of discriminatory powers in the planning and regulation of our physical, economic, and social environment. Its power and authority have become increasingly centralized and monopolistic as state and local governments have become increasingly agents of federal policies and priorities. In short, the power of government to exploit particular groups or classes of citizens is considerably greater than was true two centuries or, for that matter, even a century ago.

Furthermore, while it is true that the scientific knowledge available to government has increased, as has the professional expertise of government, it is also true that government finds itself increasingly involved in more areas of activity less susceptible to precise scientific analysis. Law enforcement has taken on the responsibility of not only apprehending and punishing criminals, but rehabilitating them. Social and economic agencies have now attempted to go beyond simply income assistance to the poor and attempt to rebuild the economic and social environments of communities and neighborhoods. Public health issues have been extended beyond the provision of sanitation and vaccination to the promotion of healthy behavior and to the protection of the environment. Park systems have gone beyond the provision of timber and recreation to the preservation of natural ecosystems. Schools have extended their purview beyond the provision of skills and social discipline to the social psychological development of children and the promotion of racial harmony. As the agenda of government has grown more ambitious, its ability to predict and control the consequences of its actions or policies has diminished.

Notwithstanding advances in the sciences, failed policies and unintended and harmful consequences seem to abound. This is particularly true where government seeks to modify human behavior, which seems still as uncertain and as unpredictable as it was when David Hume, Adam Smith, Alexander Hamilton, and James Madison recorded their observations on human nature. The type of social science requisite to our ambitious agenda of government has not always been forthcoming. Therefore, the potential for unintended harm and exploitation of citizens, as a result of government actions, is at least as great as it was for our relatively uninformed and unenlightened eighteenth and nineteenth century ancestors and probably much greater. The need to protect citizens from the uncertain consequences of discretionary power remains strong.

Finally, while comparisons of the climate of political opinion with the eighteenth and nineteenth centuries are obviously problematic, if not impossible, it would be difficult to argue that we live during a particularly harmonious era in terms of our social and political opinions. As noted, in chapter one, there seems to be an increasing ideological dissensus in public perceptions and attitudes. This increasing diversity of perceived interests and rights and divergence of visions of the public good increase the danger that some groups in society may use government to promote either their interests or their narrow vision of the public good at the expense of others. The factionalism, which Madison thought the greatest danger to our republic, is obviously still very much with us and its effects still need to be checked.

Far from losing its relevance then, the anti-rationalist vision of government still seems quite germane to these times. In a large centralized government, capable of exercising extensive discriminatory power and pressured by conflicting factions, it still would seem a good idea to check the abuse of power. It follows then that the anti-rationalist vision of public administration is also relevant to our times and should not be dismissed as a product of once fashionable but now outmoded ideas. This is not to suggest that the rationalist notion of public administration as an instrument of the common good or general will is irrelevant. Attempts to design a more rational business-like public administration, one that is more responsive to informed political leadership and less hemmed in by rules and procedures, may very well have considerable value when applied to smaller subnational units of government. Here, the powers of government are more limited, interests and preferences may be less diverse and, in any case, many citizens at least can exert the option of "voting with their feet" and leaving the jurisdiction of governments they perceive as exploitative. However, at least at the national level of government, a more anti-rationalist vision would seem appropriate.

ANTI-RATIONALISM IN THE ADMINISTRATIVE STATE

The anti-rationalist vision of public administration presented here is, of course, normative rather than positive. It suggests what an anti-rationalist public administration ought to look like rather than what American public administration does look like. Nonetheless, despite its imperfections, some of the characteristics of the modern American administrative state at least approximate the anti-rationalist vision of public administration.

The anti-rationalist vision of public administration emphasizes the necessity of administrative discretion as a check on the power of political leaders. Writings on the American administrative state make it clear that public administrators in the federal bureaucracy are able in fact to exercise considerable discretion in responding to the directives of political leaders. They are not simply instruments to be used at will by political leaders. As James Q. Wilson (1989), for example, has observed, "Congress is almost never a 'principal' that can give unchallenged direction to its 'agent,' the bureaucracy" (237). Neither is the bureaucracy in Wilson's view the "helpless pawn of whatever control measures the president seeks to put in place" (274). Rather, as he notes, the bureaucracy "can maneuver among its many political masters in ways that displease some of them and can define its tasks for internal reasons and not simply in response to external demands" (237). Consistent with an anti-rationalist view of public administration, public administrators in the modern administrative state do exercise discretion by choosing among their political masters. What the anti-rationalist vision of public administration suggests is that this discretion is not necessarily bad but rather may be required if public administrators are to check the power of political leaders.

At the same time, however, it is clear that the discretion exercised by public administrators in the modern administrative state is significantly constrained by administrative rules and procedures. These include the extensive use of line-item budgets, civil service personnel regulations, procurement regulations, due process regulations, and so on. Wilson (1989) argues that we rely "on rules to control the exercise of official judgement to a greater extent than any other industrialized democracy" (342). He also observes that "rule-bound administration" is a "our natural posture" (335). Steven Kelman (1987) notes similarly that "no other country in the world prescribes such a detailed set of decision-making procedures for government agencies" (97). While these rules and procedures are often criticized as unnecessary "red tape" and have prompted concern and criticism in some quarters (Osborne and Gaebler 1993; National Performance Review 1993), an anti-rationalist perspective would suggest that they are important in checking the exercise of administrative discretion. If American public administrators are to exercise significant policy discretion in responding to the directives of their political leaders, rules and procedures would seem necessary to limit the abuse of that discretion.

Finally, it is clear that the modern administrative state does encourage considerable participation by citizens in administrative decision making. Kelman (1987) notes the "panoply of public hearings" and "cross-examination of witnesses" peculiar to the American administrative state and observes that "few countries require anything resembling the openness of the American process" (97). Wilson (1989) argues that, while "we have a system laden with rules," we also have "a system suffused with participation: advisory boards, citizen groups, neighborhood councils, congressional investigators, crusading journalists, and lawyers serving writs" (377). As a result, Wilson concludes that the administrative state is "rule-bound without being overpowering, participatory without being corrupt" (377). This openness of the administrative state to broad citizen participation means that citizens have significant opportunities to provide information and to voice their opinions and objections to administrative decisions, and makes it more likely that those opinions and objections will be taken into account by administrators.

All this is not to suggest that the modern administrative state embodies completely the anti-rationalist vision of public administration. As Kenneth Culp Davis (1969) has argued, there may well be a good case for more extensive rule making and improved appeal processes to further protect citizens from the abuse of administrative discretion. My point here is simply that public administrators today exercise a type of constrained discretion that is at least broadly consistent with an anti-rationalist vision of public administration. To this extent, the modern administrative state has evolved in a manner that reflects an anti-rationalist worldview. Furthermore, the opportunities for checking political power within the administrative state, whatever its source, would seem to conform to the spirit, if not the letter, of the Founders' writings. If this is correct then, the administrative state warrants perhaps a greater degree of legitimacy than its critics have maintained.

A good question may be raised here as to whether or not the significant anti-rationalist elements in our administrative state can over time survive attempts by various political leaders to render public administration a more efficient and responsive instrument of their political will. I must admit to some concern here, but there is cause for at least cautious optimism. Firstly, because of our constitutional separation of powers, attempts by any one branch of government to secure substantially greater control over the administrative state are likely to be resisted by other branches of government, if only because the latter branches will not easily give up their own power over administration. Congress, for example, has historically resisted and circumvented repeated attempts by presidents to use administrative reform to reduce its role in the administration of agencies (Wilson 1989). Secondly, while most citizens do not love the administrative state, neither do they seem terribly enthusiastic about radically reforming it. Indeed, in recent times, citizens have typically exhibited far more enthusiasm for constitutional reforms, directed at checking the discretionary power of elected leaders, than they have for administrative reforms, directed at making administration more responsive to particular groups of political leaders. In this respect, citizens may perhaps have a better appreciation than many academicians and administrative experts for what the Founders were seeking to do.

TOWARD A NEW PERSPECTIVE

If we wish to preserve and enhance the anti-rationalist character of the administrative state, public administration writers themselves would do well to begin to demonstrate a better appreciation of and sympathy toward the worldview of the Founders. As public administration writers, we need to ask ourselves what kind of administrative state we would like to see in a world in which human reason is limited and prone to error; a world in which men and women lack the knowledge to consciously design and run a social order; a world in which government is often the instrument of passions and interests; and a world in which progress is linked to the development of rules that limit the harm we can do to each other, not only in our private interactions but also in our political interactions. We need to realize that power may be wielded, not only by those who may be sympathetic to the interests and values we may happen to favor, but also by those who may be indifferent or even hostile to them, and to ask then what this implies for a desirable type of public administration.

In other words, we need, like the Founders, to see the world somewhat more in anti-rationalist terms. This does not mean that we should be content with the status quo in administration and not seek improvement. It does, however, suggest that, in seeking to improve administration, we need to acknowledge the inevitable fallibility of the political and administrative process and the dangers of inadequately restraining political and administrative power. We should not seek to design an administrative state for operation by omniscient saints. We should be skeptical of those who seek a more efficient and entrepreneurial administrative state without regard to its potential dangers. As we evaluate the administrative state and suggest reforms, we need to add the potential for checking the abuse of power to our existing criteria of efficiency and effectiveness in administration. In doing so, we may then move closer toward a public administration more consistent with our political heritage and one more deserving of legitimacy.

We need also to bring the anti-rationalist perspective on government and public administration more explicitly to the attention of our own public administration students, who either are already practitioners or aspire to be such. In this respect, perhaps the most lamentable feature of contemporary public administration education is the lack of attention typically given to constitutionalism. As Donald Maletz (1991) has argued, there is, in public administration writings, "a long established tendency to gloss over constitutionalism . . . which has helped to shape an approach to administrative education that gives the study of constitutional practice a very marginal role" (375). Students of public administration need to have an understanding and appreciation of the worldview that underlies our constitutional system of government in which they act, and to explore the implications of this worldview for their role in the process of governance. In this respect, I believe they should at a minimum be encouraged to examine and discuss the work of the Founders and its implications for public administration. Some exposure here to the writings of John Locke, David Hume, Adam Smith, Adam Ferguson, Edmund Burke, and other anti-rationalists and an examination of their relevance to contemporary public administration would frankly also have value. Even the work of Friedrich Hayek, an outspoken critic of government and bureaucracy, can be shown to have considerable relevance in thinking constructively about the practice of public administration (Spicer 1993).

In conclusion, I should emphasize that the anti-rationalist vision of public administration advanced in this work may not be the only or even the best way of linking a vision of public administration to the anti-rationalist worldview of the Founders. As one sympathetic to the anti-rationalist worldview, I must concede that my own perceptions are imperfect and subjective and that other interpretations are no doubt possible. My hope, primarily, is that this work may prompt a reexamination of the anti-rationalist worldview expressed by the Founders and its relevance to contemporary public administration. If we can at least debate competing visions of public administration in terms of the Founders' worldview, then to the extent that we can come to a consensus about what is or at least what is not a desirable public administration, it will be one rooted in our political tradition rather than one that is indifferent or even antagonistic to that tradition.

References

Acton, Lord, 1986. *Essays in the History of Liberty.* Indianapolis: Liberty Press.

Adams, Guy B., 1992. "Enthralled with Modernity: The Historical Context of Knowledge and Theory Development in Public Administration." *Public Administration Review,* 52: 363–373.

Adams, Guy B., Priscilla V. Bowerman, Kenneth M. Dolbeare, and Camilla Stivers, 1990. "Joining Purpose to Practice: A Democratic Identity for the Public Service." In Henry D. Kass and Bayard L. Catron (eds.), *Images and Identities in Public Administration.* Newbury Park, Calif.: Sage Publications.

Appleby, Paul H., 1945. *Big Democracy.* New York: Alfred A. Knopf.

Beard, Charles A., 1941. *An Economic Interpretation of the Constitution of the United States.* New York: Free Press.

Bentham, Jeremy, 1962. *The Works of Jeremy Bentham, Volume 9.* New York: Russell and Russell.

Brennan, Geoffrey, and James Buchanan, 1985. *The Reason of Rules.* Cambridge: Cambridge University Press.

Buchanan, James M., 1975. *The Limits of Liberty: Between Anarchy and Leviathan.* Chicago: University of Chicago Press.

_____, 1979. *What Should Economists Do?* Indianapolis: Liberty Press.

Buchanan, James, and Gordon Tullock, 1962. *The Calculus of Consent.* Ann Arbor: University of Michigan Press.

Burke, Edmund, 1955. *Reflections on the French Revolution.* Indianapolis: Bobbs-Merrill.

_____, 1968. *Edmund Burke: Selected Writings and Speeches.* Gloucester, Mass.: Doubleday.

_____, 1992. *Further Reflections on the Revolution in France.* Indianapolis: Liberty Press.

_____, 1993. *Pre-Revolutionary Writings.* Cambridge: Cambridge University Press.

Burke, John P., 1986. *Bureaucratic Responsibility.* Baltimore: John Hopkins University Press.

Caldwell, Lynton, 1976. "Novus Ordo Seclorum: The Heritage of American Public Administration." *Public Administration Review,* 36: 476–488.

Catron, Bayard L., and Michael M. Harmon, 1981. "Action Theory in Practice." *Public Administration Review,* 41: 535–541.

Comte, Auguste, 1974. *The Positive Philosophy.* New York: AMS Press.

Condorcet, Antoine-Nicolas de, 1955. *Sketch for a Historical Picture of the Progress of the Human Mind.* New York: Noonday Press.

Cook, Brian J., 1992. "Subordination or Independence for Administrators? The Decision of 1789 Reexamined." *Public Administration Review,* 52: 497–503.

Davis, Kenneth Culp, 1969. *Discretionary Justice.* Baton Rouge: Louisiana State University.

Denhardt, Robert D., 1981. "Toward a Critical Theory of Public Administration." *Public Administration Review,* 41: 628–635.

Dewey, John, 1935. *Liberalism and Social Action.* New York: G. P. Putnam's Sons.

_____, 1939. *Freedom and Culture.* New York: Capricorn Books.

_____, 1947. "Morals and Conduct." In Saxe Commins and Robert N. Linscott (eds.), *Man and Man: The Social Philosophers.* New York: Random House.

DiIulio, John J., Jr., 1989. "Recovering the Public Management Variable: Lessons from Schools, Prisons, and Armies." *Public Administration Review,* 49: 127–133.

Dimock, Marshall E., 1936. "The Criteria and Objectives of Public Administration." In John M. Gaus, Leonard D. White, and Marshall E. Dimock, *The Frontiers of Public Administration.* Chicago: University of Illinois Press.

Downs, Anthony, 1967. *Inside Bureaucracy.* Boston: Little, Brown.

Eskridge, William, 1988. "Politics without Romance: Implications of Public Choice Theory for Statutory Interpretation." *Virginia Law Review,* 74: 275–338.

Ferguson, Adam, 1980. *An Essay on the History of Civil Society.* New Brunswick, N.J.: Transaction Publishers.

Finer, Herman, 1925. "The Civil Service in the Modern State." *American Political Science Review,* 19: 277–289.

_____, 1941. "Administrative Responsibility in Democratic Government." *Public Administration Review,* 1: 335–350.

Fisher, Louis, 1987 "The Administrative World of Chadha and Bowsher." *Public Administration Review,* 47: 213–219.

Fox, Charles J., and Clarke E. Cochrane, 1990. "Discretionary Public Administration: Toward a Platonic Guardian Class?" In Henry D. Kass and Bayard L. Catron (eds.), *Images and Identities in Public Administration.* Newbury Park, Calif.: Sage Publications.

Frederickson, H. George, 1971. "Toward a New Public Administration." In Frank Marini (ed.), *Toward a New Public Administration: The Minnowbrook Perspective.* Scranton: Chandler Publishing.

_____, 1990. "Public Administration and Social Equity." *Public Administration Review,* 50: 228–237.

Frederickson, H. George, and David K. Hart, 1985. "The Public Service and the Patriotism of Benevolence." *Public Administration Review,* 45: 547–553.

Freedman, James O., 1978. *Crisis and Legitimacy: The Administrative Process and American Government.* Cambridge: Cambridge University Press.

Friedrich, Carl J., 1940. "Public Policy and the Nature of Administrative Responsibility." In Carl J. Friedrich (ed.), *Public Policy.* Cambridge: Harvard University Press.

Golembiewski, Robert T., 1992. "Excerpts from 'Organization as a Moral Problem.'" *Public Administration Review,* 52: 95–98.

Goodnow, Frank, 1900. *Politics and Administration.* New York: Russell and Russell.

Goodsell, Charles T., 1985. *The Case for Bureaucracy: A Public Administration Polemic.* 2nd ed. Chatham, N.J.: Chatham House Publishers.

Gulick, Luther, and Lyndall Urwick (eds.), 1937. *Papers on the Science of Administration.* New York: Institute of Public Administration.

Hart, David K., 1974. "Social Equity, Justice and the Equitable Administrator." *Public Administration Review*, 34: 3–11.

_____, 1989. "A Partnership in Virtue among all Citizens." *Public Administration Review*, 49: 101–114.

Haveman, Robert H., and Julius Margolis (eds.), 1983. *Public Expenditure and Policy Analysis*. Boston: Houghton-Mifflin Company.

Hayek, Friedrich A., 1944. *The Road to Serfdom*. Chicago: University of Chicago Press.

_____, 1948. *Individualism and Economic Order*. Chicago: University of Chicago Press.

_____, 1960. *The Constitution of Liberty*. Chicago: University of Chicago Press.

_____, 1973. *Law, Legislation and Liberty, Volume 1: Rules and Order*. Chicago: University of Chicago Press.

_____, 1976. *Law, Legislation and Liberty, Volume 2: The Mirage of Social Justice*. Chicago: University of Chicago Press.

_____, 1979a. *The Counter-Revolution of Science: Studies on the Abuse of Reason*. Indianapolis: Liberty Press.

_____, 1979b. *Law, Legislation and Liberty, Volume 3: The Political Order of a Free People*. Chicago: University of Chicago Press.

Hegel, G. W., 1947. "Philosophical History." In Saxe Commins and Robert N. Linscott (eds.), *Man and the State: The Political Philosophers*. New York: Random House.

_____, 1952. *Philosophy of Right*. Translated by T. M. Cox. New York: Oxford University Press.

Heiner, Ronald, A., 1983. "The Origin of Predictable Behavior." *American Economic Review*, 73: 560–595.

Hume, David, 1984. *A Treatise of Human Nature*. New York: Penguin Books.

_____, 1987. *Essays, Moral, Political and Literary*. Indianapolis: Liberty Classics.

Kass, Henry D., 1990. "Stewardship as a Fundamental Element in Images of Public Administration." In Henry D. Kass and Bayard L. Catron (eds.), *Images and Identities in Public Administration*. Newbury Park, Calif.: Sage Publications.

Kass, Henry D., and Bayard L. Catron (eds.), 1990. *Images and Identities in Public Administration*. Newbury Park, Calif.: Sage Publications.

Kaufman, Herbert, 1977. *Red Tape: Its Origins, Uses, and Abuses*. Washington, D.C.: Brookings Institution.

_____, 1981. "Fear of Bureaucracy: A Raging Pandemic." *Public Administration Review*, 41: 1–9.

Kelman, Steven, 1987. *Making Public Policy: A Hopeful View of American Government*. New York: Basic Books.

Ketcham, Ralph (ed.), 1986. *The Anti-Federalist Papers and the Constitutional Convention Debates*. New York: Mentor Books.

Kristol, Irving, 1987. "The Spirit of '87." *The Public Interest*, 86: 3–9.

Levi, Edward H., 1949. *An Introduction to Legal Reasoning*. Chicago: University of Chicago Press.

Lindblom, Charles E., 1959. "The Science of Muddling Through." *Public Administration Review*, 29: 79–88.

_____, 1990. *Inquiry and Change: The Troubled Attempts to Understand and Shape Society*. New Haven: Yale University Press.

Locke, John, 1939a. "An Essay Concerning Human Understanding." In Edwin A. Burtt (ed.), *The English Philosophers from Bacon to Mill.* New York: The Modern Library.

———, 1939b. "An Essay Concerning the True Original, Extent, and End of Civil Government." In Edwin A. Burtt (ed.), *The English Philosophers from Bacon to Mill.* New York: The Modern Library.

Long, Norton E., 1949. "Power and Administration." *Public Administration* Review, 9: 257–264.

———, 1993. "The Ethics and Efficacy of Resignation in Public Administration." *Administration and Society*, 25: 3–11.

Lowi, Theodore J., 1979. *The End of Liberalism: The Second Republic of the United States.* 2nd ed. New York: W.W. Norton and Company.

Maletz, Donald J., 1991. "The Place of Constitutionalism in the Education of Public Administrators." *Administration and Society*, 23: 374–394.

Merriam, Charles E., 1941. *On the Agenda of Democracy.* Cambridge: Harvard University Press.

Mill, John Stuart, 1972. *Utilitarianism, On Liberty and Considerations on Representative* Government. London: J.M. Dent and Sons.

———, 1988. *The Logic of the Moral Sciences.* LaSalle, Ill.: Open Court.

Mitchell, Terence R., and William G. Scott, 1987. "Leadership Failures, the Distrusting Public and Prospects of the Administrative State." *Public Administration Review*, 47: 445–452.

Moe, Ronald C., 1990. "Traditional Organizational Principles and the Managerial Presidency." *Public Administration Review*, 50: 129–140.

Moe, Terry M., 1984. "The New Economics of Organization." *American Journal of Political Science*, 28: 739–777.

Mosher, Frederick C. (ed.), 1976. *Basic Documents of American Public Administration, 1776–1950.* New York: Howard and Meier Publishers.

Nathan, Richard P., 1976. "The Administrative Presidency." *The Public Interest*, 44: 40–54.

National Commission on the Public Service, 1989. *Leadership for America: Rebuilding the Public Service.* Washington, D.C.: Privately printed.

National Performance Review, 1993. *Creating a Government that Works Better and Costs Less.* Washington, D.C.: U.S. Government Printing Office.

North, Douglass C., 1990. *Institutions, Institutional Change and Economic Performance.* Cambridge: Cambridge University Press.

Oakeshott, Michael, 1991. *Rationalism in Politics and Other Essays.* Indianapolis: Liberty Press.

Osborne, David, and Ted Gaebler, 1993. *ReInventing Government: How the Entrepreneurial Spirit Is Transforming the Public Sector.* New York: Penguin Books.

Ostrom, Vincent, 1979. *The Intellectual Crisis in American Public Administration.* Revised Edition. Tuscaloosa: University of Alabama Press.

Overman, E. Sam, 1984. "Public Management: What's New and Different?" *Public Administration Review*, 44: 275–278.

Perry, James L. 1989. *Handbook of Public Administration.* San Francisco: Jossey-Bass.

Polanyi, Michael, 1951. *The Logic of Liberty.* Chicago: University of Chicago Press.

Polanyi, Michael, and Harry Prosch, 1975. *Meaning.* Chicago: University of Chicago.

Popper, Karl R., 1966a. *The Open Society and its Enemies, Volume 1: The Spell of Plato.* Princeton: Princeton University Press.

_____, 1966b. *The Open Society and Its Enemies, Volume 2: The High Tide of Prophecy: Hegel, Marx, and the Aftermath.* Princeton: Princeton University Press.

Rawls, John, 1971. *A Theory of Justice.* Cambridge: Harvard University Press.

Rohr, John A., 1978. *Ethics for Bureaucrats: An Essay on Law and Values.* New York: Marcel Dekker.

_____, 1986. *To Run a Constitution.* Lawrence: University Press of Kansas.

_____, 1993. "Toward a More Perfect Union." *Public Administration Review,* 53: 246–249.

Rosen, Bernard, 1983. "Effective Continuity of U.S. Government Operations in Jeopardy." *Public Administration Review,* 43: 383–392.

Rourke, Francis E., 1992. "Responsiveness and Neutral Competence in American Bureaucracy." *Public Administration Review,* 52: 539–546.

Rousseau, Jean-Jacques, 1987. *The Basic Political Writings.* Translated by Donald A. Cress. Indianapolis: Hackett Publishing.

Satori, Giovanni, 1962. "Constitutionalism: A Preliminary Discussion." *American Political Science Review,* 56: 853–864.

Schick, Allen, 1966. "The Road to PPB: The Stages of Budget Reform." *Public Administration Review,* 26: 243–258.

Schultze, Charles L., 1968. *The Politics and Economics of Public Spending.* Washington, D.C.: Brookings Institution.

Sedgwick, Jeffrey L., 1987. "Of Centennials and Bicentennials: Reflections on the Foundations of American Public Administration." *Administration and Society,* 19: 285–308.

Selznick, Philip, 1949. *TVA and the Grass Roots.* Berkeley: University of California Press.

Shangraw, R. F., Jr., and Michael M. Crow, 1989. "Public Administration as a Design Science." *Public Administration Review,* 49: 153–158.

Simon, Herbert M., 1945. *Administrative Behavior.* New York: Macmillan.

Smith, Adam, 1937. *The Wealth of Nations.* New York: The Modern Library.

_____, 1982. *The Theory of Moral Sentiments.* Indianapolis: Liberty Classics.

Sowell, Thomas, 1987. *A Conflict of Visions: Ideological Origins of Political Struggles.* New York: William Morrow.

Spencer, Herbert, 1982. *The Man Versus the State: With Six Essays on Government, Society, and Freedom.* Indianapolis: Liberty Press.

Spicer, Michael W., 1993. "On Friedrich Hayek and Public Administration." *Administration and Society,* 25: 46–59.

Stever, James A., 1988. *The End of Administration: Problems of the Profession in the Post-Progressive Era.* Dobbs Ferry, N.Y.: Transactions Publishers.

Stillman, Richard J. II (ed.), 1987. "Symposium: The American Constitution and the Administrative State (Special Issue)." *Public Administration Review,* 47.

_____, 1989. "Ostrom on the Federalist Reconsidered," *Public Administration Review,* 49: 82–84.

_____, 1991. *Preface to Public Administration.* New York: St. Martin's Press.

Taylor, Frederick W., 1985. *The Principles of Scientific Management.* Easton, Pa.: Hive.

Thompson, Dennis F., 1992. "Paradoxes of Government Ethics." *Public Administration Review*, 52: 254–259.

Thompson, Victor A., 1975. *Without Sympathy or Enthusiasm: The Problem of Administrative Compassion*. Tuscaloosa: University of Alabama Press.

Tocqueville, Alexis de, 1969. *Democracy in America*. Translated by George Lawrence. New York: Harper and Row.

Waldo, Dwight, 1984. *The Administrative State*. New York: Holmes and Meier.

Wamsley, Gary L., 1990. "The Agency Perspective: Public Administrators as Agential Leaders." In Gary L. Wamsley, Charles T. Goodsell, John A. Rohr, Philip S. Kronenburg, Orion F. White, Camilla Stivers, and Robert N. Bacher, 1990. *Refounding Public Administration*. Newbury Park, Calif.: Sage Publications.

Wamsley Gary L., Charles T. Goodsell, John A. Rohr, Philip S. Kronenburg, Orion F. White, Camilla Stivers, and Robert N. Bacher, 1990. *Refounding Public Administration*. Newbury Park, Calif.: Sage Publications.

Warren, Kenneth, 1993. "We Have Debated Ad Nauseum the Legitimacy of the Administrative State—But Why?" *Public Administration Review*, 53: 257–261.

Weber, Max, 1947. *The Theory of Social and Economic Organization*. New York: Macmillan.

White, Jay D., 1990. "Images of Administrative Reason and Rationality: The Recovery of Practical Discourse." In Henry D. Kass and Bayard L. Catron (eds.), *Images and Identities in Public Administration*. Newbury Park, Calif.: Sage Publications.

White, Leonard D., 1926. *Introduction to the Study of Public Administration*. New York: Macmillan.

Wildavsky, Aaron, 1979. *Speaking Truth to Power: The Art and Craft of Policy Analysis*. Boston: Little, Brown.

——————, 1988. "Ubiquitous Anomie: Public Service in an Era of Ideological Dissensus." *Public Administrative Review*, 48: 753–755.

Willbern, York, 1984. "Types and Levels of Public Morality." *Public Administration Review*, 44: 102–108.

Williams, Bernard, 1967. "Rationalism." *The Encyclopedia of Philosophy, Volume 7*. New York: Macmillan.

Willoughby, W. F., 1927. *Principles of Public Administration*. Washington, D.C.: Brookings Institution.

Wills, Garry (ed.) 1982. *The Federalist Papers by Alexander Hamilton, James Madison and John Jay*. New York: Bantam Books.

Wilson, James Q., 1989. *Bureaucracy: What Government Agencies Do and Why They Do It*. New York: Basic Books.

Wilson, Woodrow, 1889. *The State: Elements of Historical and Practical Problems*. Boston: D.C. Heath.

——————, 1955. *The Study of Public Administration*. Washington, D.C.: Public Affairs Press.

——————, 1956, *Congressional Government*. Cleveland: Meridian Books.

Wolin, Sheldon S., 1954. "Hume and Conservatism." *American Political Science Review*, 48: 999–1016.

Index

abuse of power, 1, 3, 5, 11, 12, 36, 39, 40, 48, 58, 59–60, 61, 63, 64, 66, 71, 73, 74, 75, 76, 80, 86, 92, 97, 98, 99, 101, 103
accountability, 8, 62, 68, 76
Acton, Lord, 48
Adams, Guy, 8, 34
administrative discretion, 11, 55–58, 60, 62, 63, 64, 65, 67–80, 81–96, 97, 98, 99, 100, 101–102
administrative responsibility, 55, 56, 57, 59, 63
administrative state, 1, 2, 4, 6, 8, 11, 40, 100–102, 103
agency theory, 31–32
Anglo-American tradition of public administration, 71–73
Anti-Federalists, 6, 38, 54
anti-rationalist public administration, 67–80, 97–104
anti-rationalist thought, 21–24
anti-rationalist worldview, xi–xii, 13, 20–24, 25, 26, 34–39, 40, 80, 93, 97, 98, 104; definition of, xi–xii, 13, 20–21
Appleby, Paul, 62
Articles of Confederation, 35

Bacon, Sir Francis, 19
Bagehot, Walter, 7
Beard, Charles, 7–8
Bentham, Jeremy, 39
bicameralism, 36, 53
Bill of Rights, 43, 53
British Constitution, 24, 34, 53
Brownlow, Louis, 29
Brutus, 38–39
Buchanan, James, 43, 94

Burke, Edmund, 21, 24, 42, 46, 49, 92, 103
Burke, John, 62, 84
business-like public administration, 2, 27, 29, 100

Cato, 39
Caldwell, Lynton, 8, 34–35
career civil service, 68–69
Catron, Bayard, 33, 58
checking power, xii, 8, 11, 12, 36, 37, 38, 39, 40, 41–53, 54, 55, 63, 64, 65, 66, 67–80, 81, 84, 89, 90, 92, 93, 95, 97, 99, 100, 101, 102, 103
chief executive, 29, 37, 61
citizen participation, 57, 63, 76–77, 78, 79, 94, 98, 101
Cochrane, Clarke, 58
common good, 14, 16, 23, 25, 33, 38, 39, 45, 94, 100
common law, 14, 89–93, 95
common will, 14, 28, 29
Comte, Auguste, 15, 17–18, 19, 31, 34
Condorcet, Antoine-Nicholas de, 15, 16–17, 18, 31, 34, 39
Congress, 62, 100, 102
consensus, 4, 93–95, 96, 98, 104
Constitution, The, xi, 5–8, 10, 11, 13, 25, 34–39, 40, 41, 53, 97. *See also* Founders, The
constitution, logic of, 41–53, 54, 97–98
constitutions, role of, 43
constrained discretion, 79–80, 90, 101
continuity, 92, 96
controls on public administration, 5, 55, 60
Cook, Brian, 79
corruption, 3, 83

right to appeal, 76
Rohr, John, 5, 6–7, 8, 39–40, 73, 83
Roosevelt, Franklin, 28
Rourke, Francis, 3
Rousseau, Jean-Jacques, 15, 16, 29, 33, 34, 50, 65
Ruckelshaus, William, 70
rule of law, 90
rules, 2, 5, 6, 7, 21, 22, 25, 46, 47, 48, 49, 73–76, 77, 78, 79, 83, 90, 92, 93, 98, 100, 101, 102

Saint-Simon, Henri de, 19
Schultze, Charles, 86
science, 2, 3, 15, 16–17, 18, 19, 20, 25, 26, 27, 28, 30, 31, 32, 56, 57, 58, 61, 63, 64, 98, 99
scientific management, 27–28, 31, 33–34
Scott, William, 1, 3, 4
Sedgwick, Jeffrey, 9
self-interest, 33, 42, 43, 44, 45, 52–53, 76. *See also* interests
Senate, 6, 36, 37, 40
separation of powers, 6, 7, 34, 36, 39, 40, 43, 50, 53, 102
Simon, Herbert, 30, 62
Smith, Adam, 21, 23–24, 81, 99, 103
social equity, 32, 84, 87–89, 95
social sciences, 3, 15, 34, 63, 99
socialism, 20, 24, 28, 30
Sowell, Thomas, 9, 12, 13
Spencer, Herbert, 49
Stever, James, 26
Stillman, Richard, 8, 26, 34, 35

Taylor, Frederick, 27
Thompson, Dennis, 83
Thompson, Victor, 88
Tocqueville, Alexis de, 48, 71–72
tradition, 14–15, 21, 24, 35, 53, 71–73, 93, 97, 104. *See also* customs
Tullock, Gordon, 94

uncertainty, 46, 91
unity of command, 68
unpredictability. *See* predictability
utilitarianism, 15, 18, 26, 27, 39, 84, 86–87, 89, 95

Waldo, Dwight, 26, 27–28, 29–30, 33–34, 86
Wamsley, Gary, 32
Warren, Kenneth, 2
Watergate, 11, 70
Weber, Max, 78–79
White, Jay, 33, 90–91
White, Leonard, 28, 30
Wildavsky, Aaron, 2–3, 32, 45
will of the people, 31, 55, 60, 61, 62, 64
Willbern, York, 43
Willoughby, W. F., 7, 28, 29, 30
Wilson, James Q., 100, 101
Wilson, Woodrow, 2, 7, 9, 27, 28, 30, 34, 61, 62, 72–73
worldview, definition of, 9–10
writers in public administration, xi, 7, 8, 9, 10–11, 13, 25, 26–34, 39, 41, 50, 53, 54–66, 69–70, 72, 73, 83, 84, 86, 87–88, 97, 98, 102